Praise for *Daydream Sunset* and Ron Jacobs

"The 'Sixties' is mostly myth and symbol now, a commodity sold in the marketplace as both cautionary tale and unattainable romance, but Ron Jacobs isn't buying it. In *Daydream Sunset*, part memoir, part lament, part impressionistic social history, he dives headfirst into the wreckage in order to paint an intimate portrait of a revolution that almost was—the widespread sense of possibility, the accelerating drive and energy, the certainty that everything old must be put on trial and anything new was worth a try, and the intoxicating soundtrack beating out the contradictory rhythms of individualism and collectivity, narcissism and social purpose."

— **Bill Ayers**, author of *Fugitive Days* and *Public Enemy*

"This is a freak's history of the 1960s and '70s told by a street active, cannabinoided participant who leaves no turn unstoned and no reactionary unscathed. Jacobs captures the era when both individual imagination and communal cooperation flourished. It's not only a glimpse into the past, but a three-dimensional map of future possibilities."

— **Michael Simmons**, *High Times* and *Mojo*

"For those who lived this life, the book will be an eye opener. We were in extraordinary times still, a cresting of the wave that changed our lives. And we rode the wave down. For the young radical, or betrayed Obama canvasser or Occupy soldier, this is crucial reading. Every page presents information for today's movements, and dazzling tales of creative dissent."

— **Paul Lacques**, I See Hawks in LA

"Ron Jacobs is a master storyteller in the tradition of Don DeLillo, unafraid to create bold and radical characters."

— **Roxanne Dunbar Ortiz**, author of *An Indigenous People's History of the United States*

"Ron Jacobs is a master who's been there, done that, and lived to tell a tale or two."

— **Ramsey Kanaan**, Publisher *PM Press*

"Jacobs's *The Way the Wind Blew*...is an accessible, readable and compelling history of their (the Weather Underground's) activities"

— **Alexander Bloom**, *Journal of American History*

"*Tripping Through the American Night*....is informative and, well, fun .... This is Jacobs' gift--his ability to describe world-historic events swirling around him in the simplest, most open-minded and most unfiltered way. "

— **Keith Rosenthal**, *Socialist Worker*

"Ron Jacobs is one of my favorite writers. "

— **Dave Zirin**, *The Nation*

Daydream Sunset

Daydream Sunset

The Sixties Counterculture in the Seventies

By Ron Jacobs

To the freaks—they know who they are

COUNTERPUNCH BOOKS

An Imprint of the Institute for the
Advancement of Journalistic Clarity

For information contact:
CounterPunch Books,
PO Box 228,
Petrolia, California. 95558.
www.counterpunch.org

Interior Design by Erik Clampitt and Nick Roney
Cover Design by Chelsea Mosher
Copyediting by Ethan Schiller
Back cover photograph to Donna Bister, 2013

Jacobs, Ron.
Daydream Sunset: the sixties counterculture in the seventies.

ISBN-13: 978-0692389614
ISBN-10: 069238961X

Contents

Foreword

You can go to the Weathermen or you can go to Vermont

By Paul Lacques

Ron Jacobs' riveting new book on 1970s counterculture will stir to life the memories of the generation that hit young adulthood as the fabled 60s waned, painfully aware that we had missed the big party.

But the 70s were vibrant and wild, an advance of the hippie/eco ethos, even as America turned indifferent and hostile to tie dye and patchouli. The Revolution didn't happen. But the deeper work began.

Jacobs' lays out the events and relationships of the decade with clarity and insight; but he slips effortlessly into the wildly optimistic, semi-crazed voice of his youth in gripping personal anecdotes.

Ron was there, and now so are you.

Made visceral are festivals and street demonstrations and riots, when sheer numbers of the young, free, and high created their own temporary community and environment, immune by sheer size to the fears of the straight world and their attempts to shut it down. There were some dangerous moments for the ruling class.

For those who lived this life, the book will be an eye opener. We were in extraordinary times still, a cresting of the wave that changed our lives. And we rode the wave down.

For the young radical, or betrayed Obama canvasser or Occupy soldier, this is crucial reading. Every page presents information for today's movements, and dazzling tales of creative dissent.

Delicate tendrils and vines have survived, yea, thrived: yippie, punk, anti-nuke, autonomen, squatter, anarchist, Green, ecofeminist, commune farmer, Metropolitan Indian, LGBT activist, comix artist, NORML, psychedelic warriors, Deadheads, underground music and art. Thrived enough to pass on their DNA.

If there is hope under these darkening skies, it is in the maturing wisdom of the counterculture living on in the young. This book lays out that wisdom so well I felt like I was understanding things about my own decade for the first time.

And so one hopes.

Paul Lacques is a songwriter and guitarist for the band "I See Hawks in LA".

Introduction

In early summer 1969 I was in a car with some friends on my way to Columbia, Maryland. The plan was to go swimming in the new indoor pool that had just opened in this model city. Our car headed out of the suburban town of Laurel, Maryland on Route 198. When we reached the spot where Route 198 intersected with US 29 we were met by a huge traffic jam. Every single car was full of young people just a couple years older than our thirteen to fifteen-year-old selves. We asked some guy hanging out a car window what was going on.

"The Who, man!" he shouted. "They're playing at Merriweather." Merriweather Post Pavilion is an outdoor amphitheater where music of all kinds is performed. Our car joined the line and I attended my first rock concert. The venue had opened the gates, although I never got closer than several thousand feet from the stage and never actually physically saw either band. The opening group was one I had never heard of: Led Zeppelin. Less than three months later they co-headlined a rock festival with Frank Zappa and the Mothers of Invention at the racetrack in my hometown. Their music would become synonymous with the upcoming decade, the 1970s. As for The Who, their rock opera *Tommy* would become one of the biggest selling albums of the year and place the band firmly in the same rock and roll stratosphere already occupied by the Rolling Stones, Bob Dylan and The Beatles.

A year later the Beatles were no more and the Rolling Stones were in the studio attempting to make sense of their free concert the previous December in Altamont, California. Bob Dylan had just released an album of standards that would be almost universally panned. Dylan didn't give a shit what the critics thought. His backup band called simply "The Band" was on the road, reaping the benefits of their first hit single "Up On Cripple Creek." I was living in Frankfurt am Main, West Germany and hung out with the hippies and hippie GIs in one of the local parks whenever I could. The US high school for military dependents featured a rock festival one weekend in April. On

May Day, protests against the US invasion of Cambodia erupted at the Goethe Universität in Frankfurt. Over 20,000 protesters marched on the US base. Naturally, the counterculture was well represented, just as it was back in the US. The protests seethed for days.

This book talks about music a lot. This is because the culture it is discussing--the counterculture--identified itself largely through the music it performed, danced and listened to, referenced and consumed. Journalist Andrew Kopkind put it concisely when he wrote in 1973, "The rock revolution may be less cataclysmic than its partisans claim, but if rock music has not detonated the social explosions of the last ten years, it has certainly transmitted them more clearly than any other media artifact."[i] More than background, the music of the 1970s counterculture was often front and center in defining the emotions, thoughts and even the actions of the adherents of that culture. The long hair of the hippie/freak culture that was dominant at the beginning of the decade to the mohawks, shaved heads and other styles that dominated the punk culture of the West's cities by the decade's end implied the preferred music of the wearer. Music not only defined style, it defined a listener's politics, drug use, and approach to life. More importantly, however, were the diminished numbers of individuals defining themselves in opposition to mainstream politics and culture of the rest of the United States. The dawning of the socially conservative New Right was at hand. Their hero was Ronald Reagan, a 1950s huckster for General Electric and a union actor who turned in his fellow union members because they were leftist. Reagan had already made a political career in California by attacking virtually every aspect of the New Left and counterculture. But he and his henchmen were just getting started.

• • •

The 1960s continue to exist as one of America's most storied and contested periods. Romanticized by young and old longing for a more innocent or revolutionary era, the period we call the Sixties is as much myth as it is truth; as much maligned as it is championed. The social and political conservatives in media and academia blame the period for everything that is wrong with today's world, despite the fact that the movement from which they sprang had its genesis during the same period as the New Left and counterculture. Indeed, today's Right is informed by the libertarian elements of the counterculture as much as today's neo-psychedelic bands are informed by their psychedelic forerunners. Neither phenomenon does its forerunner justice.

I came of age during the period discussed in this book. I turned fifteen in 1970 and twenty-five in 1980. I missed the draft by a few months, but had many friends who got caught in that snare, with a few of them actually ending up in Vietnam. My father spent 1969 and part of 1970 in Da Nang. I hated the war and the culture it represented. Of course, I wasn't alone.

This is a short impressionistic history of the Sixties counterculture's existence in the 1970s. Most of what is written here regards the United States, primarily because that is where the counterculture originated and flourished. The time covered is approximately 1970-1980, give or take a few months either way.

. . .

Gonzo writer and counterculture scribe Hunter S. Thompson once described the 1960s as a time when, "There was a fantastic universal sense that whatever we were doing was right, that we were winning... And that, I think, was the handle — that sense of inevitable victory over the forces of Old and Evil. Not in any mean or military sense; we didn't need that. Our energy would simply PREVAIL. There was no point in fighting — on our side or theirs. We had all the momentum; we were riding the crest of a high and beautiful wave..." Unfortunately, lamented Thompson, "...now, less than five years later, you can go up on a steep hill in Las Vegas and look West, and with the right kind of eyes you can almost see the high water mark — that place where the wave finally broke, and rolled back."[ii] Songwriter Jackson Browne had a similar understanding of the disintegration of the counterculture. His, too, was both apocalyptic and lyrical. Browne's three song cycle of "For Everyman," "Before the Deluge," and "The Pretender," appears on three successive discs and is the story of a generation and a culture trying to change the world while facing an apocalypse of war and environmental devastation, and, ultimately, acceding to the hegemony of the world and the system it tried so hard to change. "The Pretender," which is the final song of the cycle is a depressing admission that the system of corporate television, war, and nine to five jobs was more powerful than the world the counterculture hoped to forge, if only because it had a more developed foundation. The song itself is a tale of surrendering to that world and numbing oneself to its reality via sex, drugs and rock and roll.

Of course, the system that the cultural and political revolutionaries wanted to change was more developed, more powerful and more insidious. Besides history and years of experience, it also had the guns, the money and the law on its side. Jim Morrison's rock and roll claim that "they got the guns, but we got the numbers"[iii] would prove to be nothing but a hopeful boast. It was a boast many believed, but it was just that, a boast. The hegemon would not be shoved aside. As far as the counterculture was concerned, it proved its intractability in the 1969 battle over Berkeley's People's Park when police killed James Rector and wounded dozens more with their buckshot and clubs. It proved it again many more times in street battles between antiestablishment youth and police across the United States. The most infamous of these incidents were the murders of students at Kent State and Jackson State in May 1970. In the face of the those lethal guns, the despair, and the energy required to maintain the struggle, the exuberance of youth was overcome by a weariness beyond their years.

In a 1976 article for *New York* magazine, author Tom Wolfe called the 1970s the "me decade."[iv] John Lennon seemed to foretell Wolfe's description in at least a general way when he sang "I just believe in me, Yoko and me" in the song "God" that appeared on his first solo album. Despite the apparently egocentric lyrics of this song, Lennon continued to engage politically and culturally, playing at a concert raising funds to free cultural revolutionary John Sinclair from a ten-year prison stint for marijuana possession. In addition, Lennon and Yoko were meeting with Yippies planning protests at the 1972 Republican Convention, originally scheduled to take place in San Diego. These latter conversations provided what might have been the final impetus for the Nixon administration to intesify its efforts aimed to deport Lennon. In light of the dual pursuits of self and political change, Lennon's uncertainty is representative of the counterculture's overall argument over which direction the movement would or should go. Lennon's uncertainty wasn't new. In 1968, he and British New Leftist John Hoyland had held an open debate in the pages of *Black Dwarf,* one of Britain's underground newspapers. The debate centered on Lennon's lyrics in the Beatles' song "Revolution No. 1" that asked listeners to "free their mind instead" and wavered on whether or not he wanted to be in or out of the revolution. Hoyland countered, arguing that one could both free their mind and the society one lived in. The two men did not resolve the question but the debate enunciated a need for some kind of synthesis between the two. It would be this struggle that would obsess the people in the maelstrom that was the counterculture.[v]

Chapter 1

Them Changes...

"Happy New Year's, man...." Jimi Hendrix was playing with his new band at the east coast's rock church, the Fillmore East. It was New Year's Eve 1969-1970, one night in a four-night engagement. There was an ugliness in the air and the counterculture was not immune. From Charlie Manson to the December murder at the Altamont rock festival and from the Justice Department to Vietnam, the shit was hitting the fan. A group of eight counterculture guerrillas, antiwar activists, pacifists and even a Black Panther were on trial for conspiracy to riot during the 1968 Democratic Convention in Chicago. Black Panther Fred Hampton was murdered in his bed by a government hit squad and the Weatherman unit had thrown a few Molotov cocktails they would characterize as ineffectual. The Chicago Conspiracy verdict was less than two months away. The Beatles album *Abbey Road* was a great listen but the cohesion of the group was rotting at the core.

The Rolling Stones had pegged the entire emotion of the time with their song "Gimme Shelter" on the new album *Let It Bleed*. War and Killing was just a shot away and it was coming to white people's hometowns. A bad moon really was rising...Reefer was in short supply, thanks to a lockdown at the Mexican border. Alcohol and harder stuff was filling in the blanks in people's brains. Thank god for the Brotherhood of Eternal Love and their orange sunshine acid. At least something was still psychedelic. Hendrix and his Band of Gypsys played a handful of tunes in two separate sets that night. The Buddy Miles song "Them Changes" expressed a certain current underlying the decennial dissonance. "My mind is going through them changes/I keep going out of my mind...." Changes were certainly coming and lots of them weren't going to be so great. The Fillmore was sold out that night. Filled with a wide assortment of counterculture freaks, wannabes and has-beens, it was rocking. Promoter Bill Graham was reportedly disappointed with the first show and inspired Hendrix to kick ass during the second one. He did. The first show wasn't too shabby either.

The band was pretty new. Personality conflicts and other

differences had finally broken up the Experience and Jimi's new group was now all black. Supposedly, the racial makeup was intentional. Hendrix had been under fire from some black nationalists concerning his white band members and had been searching for suitable musicians to form a new band with. Billy Cox and Buddy Miles fit the bill nicely. Indeed, Hendrix and Cox had played together when both were in the US Army. An album was released a few months later that featured excerpts from those New Year's Eve shows. As it turned out, the ensemble would last less than a month more. Four months later, Hendrix and another band that featured Cox and Experience drummer Mitch Mitchell would play one of Hendrix's last concerts in the United States.

This concert would be memorialized in the film *Jimi Plays Berkeley*. Barely a month after the US invasion of Cambodia, Hendrix performed at the Berkeley Community Theater as thousands rioted and marched in the streets outside. This being Berkeley, the level of political rage had sustained the anger at both the invasion and the subsequent murder of at least six students in the protests that followed long after demonstrations in other cities and towns around the country had died down. In addition, the fact that there were many who did not get into the Hendrix show and felt they should have added to the sense of outrage. Hendrix and the band had little or no knowledge of the latter aspect of the riots outside, however.

The Grateful Dead, a band that served as a sometimes willing and more recently, unwilling spiritual leader and lyrical commentator on the infant counterculture, was hard at work recording two albums that would define not only much of their 1970s outlook, but also the mixed messages that had been coming down the psychedelic pike since that fateful and dramatic year 1968. If there was one message that had become clear during that traumatic annum, it was that the defenders of the status quo—with its wars, racial hatred and just plain unhipness—were not going to give up their rule without a major fight. The growing awareness of this truth was the reason for a good deal of debate amongst those attempting to change that world, culturally, politically or both. One result was a trend toward self-reflection. The politicos would call it self-criticism. Sometimes this phenomenon was nothing more than navel-gazing while at other times it seemed a genuine attempt to truly figure out how to move ahead.

An example of the latter can be found in Ed McClanahan's essay on the Altamont concert. McClanahan, who was a friend and colleague of Ken Kesey, Robert Stone and a number of other writers who came together under the auspices of Stanford University's Wallace Stegner Fellowship and had gone on to help create the San Francisco psychedelic scene from their bohemian Palo Alto neighborhood called Perry Lane, used the Grateful Dead song "New Speedway Boogie" for his essay. This song, with lyrics written by the Dead songwriter Robert Hunter, discussed the Altamont event in terms of the growing pains of a new culture. McClanahan's take on the song and the events it described can be summed up in this excerpt from the essay:

> "Robert Hunter (Grateful Dead lyricist).....does not agree that the quest after salvation—the voyage that began in the Haight Ashbury and carried us all the way to Woodstock—has dead-ended in the molten yellow hills of California just twenty miles east of where it started, impaled on the point of a Hells Angels rusty blade...Rather, the poet suggests, the journey has only just begun, and the way is long and arduous and fraught with peril."[vi]

As the 1968 Chicago riots, the May 1968 French Rebellion and the 1968 Olympics were to politics, the December 1969 Altamont concert that featured the Rolling Stones as a headliner and resulted in the death of a black concertgoer by a few drunk and wasted Hell's Angels was a bellwether event in the counterculture. The killing and general darkness surrounding the concert forced many in the counterculture to question where their Aquarian movement was truly heading. The Grateful Dead, fulfilling their role as both chronicles and philosophers of the culture, wrote not one but two songs about the events of that day.

But what was the counterculture? To the casual observer it might be described thusly. It was a primarily white, originally middle-class, and relatively well-educated phenomenon that grew out of the "Beat movement." Not nearly as dark as certain elements of the Beat culture, it could be figuratively stated that the counterculture's naiveté was reflected in the bright colors worn by many of its adherents. Instead of speed and alcohol as drugs of choice like the Beats, the new psychedelic compound LSD served as the Eucharist. Both groups shared a fondness for marijuana. The desire to reject what the Beats called square remained, yet there seemed to be no intentional plan to replace it by anything "hip." Instead, what transpired was a frustrated attempt to create a community while allowing plenty of avenues for individual expression. As it turned out, the community element diminished while the individualist aspect grew more assertive. In the hyper- capitalist society that the US was becoming, this should be no surprise. Capitalism encourages individualism. The more atomized a society becomes, the more the market expands. For example, when US families were large and extended, with many members living on the same property, many of the consumer goods that existed could be shared; when the nuclear family became the standard, more households meant more sales. Finally, in the world of the early twenty-first century, each individual has their own phone, their own device to watch video and listen to music, their own automobile, and so on. Furthermore, the way things turned out in this regard exemplifies the hegemony of that system. In other words, those determined to establish and maintain oppositional communities were up against a societal context that denied the importance of those types of community in favor of the aforementioned hyper-individualism.

By the early 1970s, elements of the counterculture could be detected in nearly every US community and in many places overseas. Its class nature had transcended its origins in the nation's middle class and was becoming part of a new working class understanding that propelled the culture out of the universities and into workplaces, bars, shopping centers and other places young people gathered. Racially, the counterculture remained an essentially white phenomenon, despite the fact it had always drawn a fair amount of its inspiration from the culture of the US black community. This was especially true in regards to the music. The peace and love ethos, while still the expressed philosophy, was up against a system that detested much of what the counterculture was perceived to be about. Long hair, drugs, an opposition to work, free sex and no morals; this was how the adult establishment saw the culture of too many of their children. And by and large adult America recoiled at what they saw. Although the right wing of the Democratic Party had done its part to express this generational disgust, especially in the streets of Chicago during their 1968 convention, Richard Nixon and his Republican Party identified and were identified with the conservative backlash against the counterculture. By 1972, the Democrats would be completely identified with the backlash's opposite.

In the late 1960s, mainstream politicians weren't the only politically-minded folks who were building campaigns around the young people running wild in the streets. So were leftist political activists like Abbie Hoffman and the leadership of the Students for a Democratic Society (SDS.) After years of police harassment over their lifestyle and the ever-looming threat of the military draft, the hippies--and those fingered by the police as such--were fighting back. The hippies were identifying themselves as "freaks,"[vii] while the political members of their generation debated about how to engage those freaks in their campaigns against the war and racism. Simultaneously, the relatively straitlaced culture of the leftist politicos had discovered marijuana and psychedelic rock music. This course of events had helped create a countercultural sensibility in SDS and also inspired some of the more anarchistic comrades to create the Yippies. By spring 1970, SDS was split into at least three different and considerably smaller groupings that included an underground faction calling themselves Weatherman (who blended counterculture practice and revolutionary politics into an angry struggle against imperialism and racism), a culturally conservative faction known as Progressive Labor, and another faction or two that were focusing their efforts on working class youth. This latter group, known originally as Revolutionary Youth Movement (RYM), had broken into smaller organizations and many represented various cultural variations on the counterculture. None were as culturally extreme as the Yippies, who placed the freak culture front and center, and none were as culturally conservative as Progressive Labor, who looked like Mormon missionaries with their short hair, jackets and ties.

Founded at a party on New Year's Eve 1967-1968 by a half dozen political activists in New York, by 1970 the Yippies were something quite different from what they had started out as. A few of the group's founders had moved on to other things: some had moved to Vermont where they helped organize a politically charged countercultural commune movement; others were dealing drugs. Abbie Hoffman was still identified with the group but the true activists in the organization were other men and women who spent their days on New York's Lower East Side and in other urban youth ghettoes around the United States. While they remained vocal in their opposition to the war, much of the Yippies' time was spent working on issues affecting the youth in their communities. In addition, a newer leadership was forming. Ultimately, members of the White Panthers and the Yippies would join together to form the Youth International Party (YIP). This party organized around housing, marijuana and drug laws, police harassment and survival. In an economy quickly transitioning from a post-scarcity economy to one based on austerity, the issue of survival was certain to become tantamount. Surviving outside of the world of regular work and rent would become even more difficult. As far as the Yippies were concerned, not having to work a regular job was essential to their existence, and therefore, so was figuring out how to do that.

Until 1971, the United States and, by default, the world economy, was dependent on the US promise to redeem dollars for gold. This was a key element of the post-World War Two Bretton Woods Agreement, and was also part of the reason gold prices were fixed at thirty-five dollars an ounce. After the economy began to contract in the early 1970s, Nixon and his cabinet decreed an end to this policy and embarked on a plan to devalue the dollar. This act alone rebalanced some of the debt that the US had accrued, mostly because of the war in Vietnam. However, the economy continued to underperform. In 1972, the Libyan government of Muammar Gaddafi nationalized its oil reserves. This caused the price of oil to increase by nearly 70 percent, an action that caused inflation for US consumers to skyrocket. In 1973, Washington ended the fixed value of gold. This caused an immediate rise in the price of gold, as well as many consumer goods. 1973 was also the year that the personal income of US workers peaked and a recession that lasted at least two years began. The recession created a situation where wages stagnated while prices of certain essentials continued to climb, further shrinking the real income of the labor force. The nation's minimum wage was stuck at $1.60 an hour. Congress would only increase that amount by a total of fifty cents an hour over the next seven years. In constant dollars, this meant that there was no real increase in the wage earner's spending power. Meanwhile, the desire of both capital and labor to increase their share of the national income only served to push prices ever higher, despite a decline in the hegemony of the US dollar in the world capitalist system. Wall Street and its associates in Washington were already setting the stage for a policy that is now known as neoliberalism.

When it came to most of America's youth, this economic situation only meant that they were going to have to find work to survive, if there was any. The age of prosperity was over for the regular folks in the US of A. With the minimum wage barely increasing at all over the decade, the prospects for the unskilled young were not good and becoming worse. Furthermore, the corporate transfer of better-paid, usually union, jobs to non-union countries was now underway. The counterculture dream of a meaningful and idyllic life was slipping further away for young working class Americans than at any time since the early 1960s. The streets were back to merely being places one hung out after work or places to hang out in place of work. Unlike the not-so-long-ago streets of their hippie predecessors, they were no longer places young adults chose to live in while trying to create a new world.

The young Bruce Springsteen knew this scenario all too well. His teen years in the Jersey shore towns of Asbury Park and Freehold introduced him to the life of the working class in a rapidly changing capitalist economy. His father, a factory worker, who like most factory workers dependent on the whims of capitalism, was occasionally unemployed. Many of Springsteen's friends were even worse off and often employed part-time or seasonally. Northern New Jersey was in the throes of a major economic shift and New York City was tumbling towards bankruptcy. Over the course of the decade, the songs Springsteen composed would shift from the colorful stories of hard luck street characters and oceanside lovers that dominated on his first two recordings to tales of escape, frustration, hopelessness and defeated love. Never a hippie, his physical appearance would change from that of an ungroomed skinny freak to a clean-cut guy who looked like the Marlboro man substituting a guitar and a song for a cigarette and a horse. The music Springsteen began to make in earnest in 1975 was music about the working people he knew. It described their despair, yet it also expressed their desires; desires that might be considered quite diminished after the headiness of young people's dreams in the 1960s.

In other words, Springsteen was not a counterculture bard. As he saw it, his place was within the greater American milieu. After all, it was what he knew best and, more importantly, what he related to best. Although the Grateful Dead had produced what several critics labeled a "hippie" album when they released *Wake of the Flood* in late 1973, just five weeks after Springsteen's *The Wild, the Innocent and the E Street Shuffle*, it seemed clear that the hippie culture the Dead represented was shrinking back from the broader world into the bohemian quarters it had originated from or it was retreating to the countryside. Springsteen's view of the nation would become the future of American music. Indeed, he had already been heralded as such by rock critic Jon Landau. The counterculture would not disappear completely, but it would never hold the attention of America's youth like it had for a few short years in the late 1960s. *Wake of the Flood*'s inspiration derived from the Northern California countryside the Dead had fled to in 1970. The album's lyrics spoke of farming and seasonal cycles. The songs on the album offered stories of country maidens and harvests. They mixed biblical images reminding the listener of the eternal cycle of death and rebirth with stories about rivers and intrepid travelers. The songs spoke about survival on both an individual and cultural level. The message seemed to be that the counterculture would exist in the country and in the minds of those who joined the traveler's caravan, if it was to survive anywhere. Another group deeply connected to the counterculture was San Francisco's Jefferson Airplane. After two electric albums (1968's *Crown of Creation* and 1969's *Volunteers*) celebrating the revolution in consciousness and calling everyone to battle, the group backed off, formed other bands (Jefferson Starship and Hot Tuna) and their revolutionary calls morphed into science fiction fantasy (*Blows Against the Empire)*, blues and rock and roll weariness (*Red Octopus*.)[viii]

In that other world of work and bills, the reality of capitalism's cyclic rollercoaster ride was rendering the post-scarcity economy moot, except for those who had never known scarcity. In other words, the rich were staying rich and everyone else was paying the cost. It was business as usual in the land of Wall Street and the Bank of America.

Besides Springsteen, there were other musicians addressing the situation of working youth. Bob Seger of Detroit is one such musician. Like Springsteen, Seger's songs told stories about family and economic despair; decaying downtowns and failed hopes. Neither artist indicated how the situation might be reversed. Those that did call for radical change were few and far between. One such band, calling itself Prairie Fire, was a musical entity that worked with the Revolutionary Union (RU)) In fact, RU helped sponsor Prairie Fire's 1974-1975 tour of fifty-four cities. Despite their musicianship, Prairie Fire's overt politics and commitment to the communist revolutionary mission almost guaranteed that their records would not be promoted as aggressively as the non-revolutionary Springsteen. It's not that both groups wrote about different situations, it was much more about how they marketed their songs. For instance, not long after Prairie Fire's tour was over in 1975, Bruce Springsteen appeared on the covers of both *Time* and *Newsweek* magazine the same week. Prairie Fire never even made the cover of the Revolutionary Union's San Francisco newspaper.

Bruce Springsteen wrote and sang about the lives of those whose work and income were inextricably tethered to the ups and downs of capitalist economics. Working people had little power when it came to expanding economic growth and, when the economy shrank, their work weeks and income shrank along with it. The Grateful Dead retold ancient myths about those who tried to live outside those cycles, yet they were also tied to their own rhythms of losing, winning, fighting and hoping. Some rock bands, echoing their brothers and sisters in the streets, made hopeful calls for cultural and political revolution. By the end of the decade, the music called punk rock lashed out at it all. Pissed off at being left with the aftermath of capitalism's post World War Two party, angry and mostly white working class kids calling themselves punks blamed the hippies, the Queen of England, the cops, and even occasionally the Blacks for their future of no future. The angriest-sounding of them all were the Sex Pistols. Their tantrum was heard around the world. It agitated the mainstream press and a multitude of others in government and the upper classes (which was part of the point.) Then, as soon as the tantrum began, it was over and everyone counted their losses. Other punk groups were neither as nihilistic nor as random in their attacks. They made music instead of headlines. Like any of their predecessors in another of rock's brief but multiple periods, no punk band would have been as successful at another time or in another place.

If there was one other rock band that appeared to live the freak life besides the Grateful Dead, it was the band Crosby, Stills, Nash & Young. Following their extremely successful debut at the Woodstock festival, the group recorded a second album titled *Déjà Vu*. The first single from the album was Joni Mitchell's poetic paean to the counterculture myth the Woodstock festival had become. The band accelerated the song's original tempo and added the rock guitar work of Stephen Stills and Neil Young, changing Mitchell's jazzy approach into a rock radio format that broke into *Billboard* magazine's top twenty. Other songs on the record reflected the changes being experienced by members of the counterculture as the generation matured and searched for a way to maintain their alternative vision.

The song "Our House" described two lovers' domestic bliss, while "Teach Your Children" offered poetic platitudes about childhood and parenthood. Joni Mitchell, too, sang of these more domestic realities.

Less than two months after *Déjà Vu*'s release, National Guard troops killed four students during an antiwar protest at Kent State University in Ohio. The protests began after President Richard Nixon announced on national television that US troops were invading Cambodia, thereby expanding the war in Southeast Asia. Within minutes of Nixon's announcement, protests broke out across the United States, with many of them taking place in university towns and villages. By the next evening, hundreds of colleges were on strike, high school students were walking out, military draftees refused to work; ROTC and other military–related buildings on campuses were set afire and civil authorities called in National Guard and reinforced their local police forces. The universality of the protests, especially among the young, did two things. It proved the broadness of the opposition to the US war in Vietnam and created a national crisis. Some establishment figures called for a retreat from the barricades while others sent fully-armed troops directly into the fray. Ohio Governor James Rhodes was of the latter camp, sending hundreds of National Guard troops to Kent, Ohio on May 2, 1970. The afternoon of May 4th, four students were dead from Guard bullets and over a dozen others were wounded, some permanently. Neil Young penned an angry song deploring the murders and the band released it as a single almost immediately. The song peaked on the *Billboard* charts at number fourteen. The introduction to the song is one of rock's most memorable guitar licks ever recorded. The song was banned on some radio stations because of its lyrical content. This included the entire Armed Forces Network (AFN) in Europe. An AFN disc jockey who ignored the ban and played the song anyhow was stripped of his radio duties and reassigned. Post Exchanges (shopping centers on military posts) pulled the record from their shelves. The band toured in late 1970 and early 1971, despite a number of personal differences exacerbated by the road and cocaine. After the tour, various members toured separately and together. They then reunited for a sold-out (despite no further new releases as a band) tour in 1974.

The Not So Merry Month of May 1970

The last days of April 1970 seemed relatively uneventful. The first Earth Day occurred on April 22nd that year. For the most part, the day was not a radical showdown with police. The most recent such episode had taken place in many US cities following the conviction of the Chicago 7 defendants in February. Over a hundred thousand members of the US radical movement were gathering the last weekend of April in New Haven to protest the trial of Black Panthers Bobby Seale and Ericka Huggins on charges they were eventually acquitted of. Even that protest was characterized as mostly peaceful.

Then April ended. Not with a whimper but a bang. The night of April 30, 1970, Richard Nixon told the world that US forces were invading Cambodia ostensibly to destroy the warmaking capabilities of the NLF and northern Vietnamese military. The speech was not even over before students and others across the US were in the streets. The protesters in New Haven issued a call for a nationwide student strike. A torrent of protest raged across the nation. In Frankfurt am Main, Germany, thousands of protesters marched on the US Army offices known as the IG Farben Building. Besides the German protesters, there were GIs refusing to work and US military dependents walking out of their schools. Black armbands expressing solidarity with the protesters and against the war could be seen on many a young person on base—GIs and dependents alike. The authorities were naturally wary. May was to be the cruelest month this calendar year.

Protests and riots raged across the nation. At the University of Maryland and dozens of other colleges and universities, authorities called in the National Guard. The bands played on, aware of the maelstrom growing all around them. No one, however, except for the perhaps the most apocalyptic members of society, saw what was coming next. On May 4, 1970, the Ohio National Guard murdered four students and wounded more than a dozen others during a protest at Kent State University.

Organizers working with the Boston-Cambridge anti-imperialist group the November Action Coalition (NAC) were among the many Boston area antiwar organizations organizing a never-ending round of protests. It seems that some NAC members were fans of the band and had the ear of the Grateful Dead. The band wanted to do something to express their state of mind about the escalation of the war. So they set up on Kresge Plaza on the MIT campus during a May 6th protest and played a nine song set.

The maelstrom of war, racism, and rebellion unleashed in the wake of Nixon's words on April 30th took at least eight more stateside victims in the weeks following that Grateful Dead concert in Cambridge, Six blacks protesting racism in Augusta, Georgia were gunned down. On May 14, 1970 two more young people were killed by Mississippi state troopers while protesting the war. The forces of law and order were resorting to the one card they could always pull from their sleeve: raw, murderous violence. Black and Brown-hued Americans knew this all too well. White ones were rediscovering it. Neither the war nor the racism of US political and cultural society was near an end.

Bob Dylan was out of the public light when the 1970s began. His *Nashville Skyline* album, released in late autumn 1969, was on the charts but not even remotely revolutionary in a political or cultural sense. Although it shared the countrified sound Dylan had introduced on his previous disc *John Wesley Harding*, it shared none of that album's apocalyptic lyrics. In fact, it was mostly forty minutes of nice country music. Those Dylan fans who looked to him for groundbreaking, even revolutionary insight were appalled. At the time, there was a cultural chasm between country-western music and rock. This had little to do with the music and much to do with the different worlds the musical forms represented. Country and western assumed the supremacy of white America, well-defined gender roles, and celebrated a lifestyle that revolved around working hard that only improved by pulling oneself up by one's bootstraps. By the end of the 1960s, these assumptions were occasionally being challenged by musicians like country star Johnny Cash and bluegrass pioneer Earl Scruggs. Furthermore, songs like Jeanie C. Riley's "Harper Valley, PTA" and Tammy Wynette's "D-I-V-O-R-C-E' seemed to represent a stronger female archetype than was usual in the genre.

Bob Dylan's next album, titled *Self Portrait*, was even less revelatory than *Nashville Skyline* as far as the public was concerned. More interesting to Dylan fans and the counterculture media were the recently released bootleg recordings collected on the disc everyone called *The Great White Wonder*. These songs came mostly from a series of light hearted recording sessions made in Woodstock, New York with the backing band from his 1965 tour. This band, which had been going by the name The Hawks, was now calling themselves The Band. Other songs on the album were from earlier sessions and live shows. I recall a local station outside of DC (WHMC) playing the album endlessly.

By 1974, Dylan was back with a vengeance. Along with *Self-Portrait*, he had released a collection of somewhat jazzy tunes titled *New Morning*. After leaving Columbia Records for the new (to Dylan and the recording industry) label Asylum, he went on tour with

The Band to plaudits and applause. Tickets were almost impossible to procure and almost everyone who attended a show went away impressed and happy that Dylan was back. The truth was he was just getting going. Over the next twenty months or so, he released two albums, *Blood On the Tracks* and *Desire*, with both of them topping his previous records in sales and encouraging critics to write happily that Dylan "was back."

For the purposes of this text, the more interesting album was *Desire*. Released in January 1976, the disc kicked off with an almost seven-minute ballad championing the cause of a boxer imprisoned under questionable circumstances. The boxer, whose name was Rubin Hurricane Carter, had been doing time in the New Jersey prison system for a murder and robbery in a bar several years previous. The details of his conviction were quite sketchy and had recently come to the attention of prison and civil rights activists, including communist groups and churches. Although the prisoner rights movement had quieted since the rebellions at Attica and other prisons earlier in the decade, there were still plenty of people advocating for justice and fair treatment.

The music on *Desire* was a masterful blend of gypsy melodies (from street violinist Scarlet Rivera), Indian rhythms, Dylan lyrics, and harmonies from future country music star Emmylou Harris and Ronee Blakely. The poet Allen Ginsberg played finger cymbals on a song or two. In the wake of the album's release, Dylan and a few of his longtime friends (musicians Joan Baez and Bobby Neuwirth foremost among them) began to organize what turned out to be the last great counterculture revival musical revue and freak show. Yes, the Grateful Dead would continue their magical mystery tour for almost two more decades, but by the time it ended, the spontaneity that defined the counterculture would be the rarity instead of the norm, at least on stage. The Dylan tour was named The Rolling Thunder Revue and had everything a countercultural traveling show could want: rock and roll, politics, drugs, tour buses, beautiful women, and a genuine Beat poet and all-around counterculture hero, Allen Ginsberg.

The tour was not just another rock band on the road. Somewhat like Leon Russell and Joe Cocker's 1970 Mad Dogs and Englishmen tour it was a traveling circus, except with a purpose. That purpose was to free Hurricane Carter and, by doing so, remind the rock and roll nation that racism in the United States had not disappeared. Indeed, it was as bad as it ever was, albeit better camouflaged. The biggest difference was that it was harder to see now that America's legal apartheid had lost its sanction, thanks to the civil rights and black liberation struggles of the previous twenty years. The other role this tour would play would be to remind the rock and roll nation that its music was more than just a goodtime sound. It was a talking drum, the manner by which the culture's message reached its adherents and the powers that be. Free Hurricane! Free our minds! Free our country! That's what the civil rights movement was all about. Unfortunately, that movement itself was in disarray. Many of its most militant and identifiable individuals and groups had been murdered or jailed—Malcolm X, Martin Luther King and several members of the Black Panthers, among others. Others had lost their way via drugs, drink, despair, and the many temptations of capitalism. Some were just plain tired. Still others had rendered themselves virtually irrelevant by picking up the gun or the bomb and going underground, occasionally making a small noise by blowing up part of a building or by robbing a bank. Those in the movement who were left and were still thinking politically were joining communist sects that seemed to spring up weekly like mushrooms after a rain. It was a dismal time in terms of the revolution.

Death of a Digger

In 1973, Emmet Grogan's book Ringolevio was published. It is a slightly egocentric social history of Grogan and the Haight-Ashbury scene during the counterculture's early years. Grogan, one of the original San Francisco Diggers that provided free food, clothing and assistance to the hippies flooding into the Haight, lived within the myth he created. He was found dead in a New York subway car less than three years after the book's publication. The cause of death was a heroin overdose. Besides representing an end to the Digger ethos, Grogan's death garnered a memorial tribute from Bob Dylan on the cover of the album Desire.

So, Dylan hit the road. By doing so, he made rock and roll relevant again. The songs on Desire and the songs the entourage played on tour seemed like more than tales of vanity, lust, and hedonistic pleasure, and the performers were on a mission of truth. Truth was important since it was an idea in pretty short supply in 1975. Richard Nixon had slimed his way out of the White House in ignominy only a few months before. Gerald Ford, the man who had been chosen to replace the resigned Nixon without even the charade of an election, sat in his place. The US war in Vietnam, which was started and sold on a series of lies and mistruths, finally ended in May 1975 with a victory for the Vietnamese. Already, that victory was being rewritten by historians and journalists with too much invested in America's non-existent exceptionalism. Somebody who was unafraid to speak (or sing in this case) the truth was sorely needed. As it turned out, Bob Dylan and the Rolling Thunder Revue would fit the bill.

Dylan was insistent on keeping the tour away from the glitz and excess big rock tours had become synonymous with. The shows on the tour were rarely announced more than two days before they were scheduled. Even then, the announcements were usually made via a loose network of FM radio stations that had pioneered the "underground" radio concept. Among these stations were WNEW in New York, WHFS in Bethesda, Maryland, KMPX in San Francisco and WBCN in Boston. All stations using this format allowed the disc jockeys to play music to their liking, ignoring the pressure from record companies or advertisers. This free form approach contrasted to the Top 50 format and the newer Album-Oriented Rock (AOR) format becoming popular as corporations bought up previously independent stations on the FM dial. Although the core of performers remained intact, several of the performers on the Rolling Thunder tour changed frequently. Dylan's muse was the spirit of the Beats, the rumble of th e road, and the Shoshone medicine man whose name the tour bore.

By the end of the decade, however, he would be a born-again Christian looking for answers to the questions he had always asked. The simplicity of the born-again message would not only diminish his musical reach and creativity, it would also decrease his fan base substantially.

The Rolling Stones, on the other hand, defined rock's glitz and excess. Not only did they define it, but by 1975, they seemed to revel in it. They weren't alone in this (Led Zeppelin was a determined rival for the crown), but since the Stones were the biggest rock band in the world after the Beatles broke up, they were the example held up for scorn and praise for this fact by critics. While Mick Jagger partied with the rich and the British aristocracy, the rest of the band enjoyed their riches, even moving to France in 1972 to avoid British taxes. They saw themselves as tax rebels, but it was difficult not to see them as just some more rich guys trying to avoid paying tax. As it turned out, the exile helped produce one of the best Rolling Stones albums ever recorded. That album, titled *Exile on Main Street*, was recorded in the basement of Keith Richards' home in southern France and blended blues, country, and rock and roll into a gritty, down-to-earth double set of disturbingly beautiful music. If there were a list of albums whose sound and lyrics encapsulated the situation of the counterculture in 1971, *Exile on Main Street* and Sly and the Family Stone's *There's a Riot Going On* would top the list. Both albums were rootsy chronicles of the counterculture's descent into narcotics, cynicism and the depression that a failed romance almost always brings. The Stones continued to make fairly good music throughout the decade, but the street credibility they had earned in the 1960s was gone by 1978. Despite Keith Richards' expressed wish that they could mount a tour like Dylan's Rolling Thunder Revue, the fact was that Keith was becoming increasingly marginalized as a creative force in the band. The Rolling Stones would never again tour as anything less than the very rich men they had become. To their credit, they would continue to champion non-rock and lesser known acts by hiring them as opening acts. In 1972, Stevie Wonder had this job. As far as many women fed up with the Stones' sexist reputation (deserved or not), Wonder proved the more appealing act on the bill. The Rolling Stones would never stay at a Motel 6 again, nor would they carry their own drugs, clothes or instruments on tour. Perhaps the only remnant of their street credibility lay in their blues-driven music and Keith Richards' junk habit. Addiction to heroin apparently still had its democratizing side effects, which remained one of its few positive attributes.

Disco and Counterculture

Disco was never a part of the counterculture dance mix. However, writing any kind of cultural history of the US in the 1970s requires at least a mention of this particular beat. Born in the funk music and gay bathhouse scene, disco depended on a slick repetitive beat and simple lyrics. It was music to dance to, not to listen to. The scene wasn't just about the music though. It was also about clothes, blow-dried hair, sex and cocaine. If there was a perfect example of how corporate capitalism could strip the soul from a cultural form and leave only the elements that could be packaged and sold, then disco would be it. The production of the John Travolta star vehicle Saturday Night Fever sealed the deal, removing any remnant of substance from disco and replacing it with the pathetic and syrupy pop of the film's white bread soundtrack.

The advent of punk rock was partially a reaction to the excess represented by "classic" rock bands like The Rolling Stones and Led Zeppelin. More importantly, punk was a reaction to the growing love affair between the wealthy, the aristocracy and some of the most popular rock musicians. This reaction was expressly stated as such in Britain and some cities in the United States. In San Francisco, punk rock bands openly challenged not only the wealth and bourgeois nature of much of rock aristocracy, but also what they perceived to be a lazy hippie drug-addled apathy that had become synonymous with the Grateful Dead and their fans. How accurate were these perceptions? Leave it to say that they were accurate enough to provoke an impassioned response among many, especially young mostly white youth, to propel the movement known as punk.

If nothing else, punk was a new antithesis to the more mainstream rock world. Like any such movement that comes about in reaction to an existing one, the proselytizers of punk were more dismissive of what came before them than they were grounded in their historical understanding. While claiming to be from the street, and therefore raw and unadulterated, most punks never acknowledged that the Rolling Stones, Grateful Dead, and many other big rock acts (The Who, Deep Purple, and so on) could also claim their origins in the streets as much as any punker.

Punk was not a homogenous genre. It varied from city to city, country to country. It remained a primarily urban phenomenon limited mostly to the English-speaking world. Most of the bands in New York were incubated in the scene emanating from the CBGB club in Manhattan's Bowery. These groups, in true American style, mostly shied away from politics. The primary theme of their lyrics was teenage alienation. This trope was often filtered through an apocalyptic drug-hazed vision with sexual twists. Three of the biggest new wave bands, The Ramones, Talking Heads, and Television, all represented different musical and lyrical sensibilities. All were lumped together with the New York Dolls, Patti Smith and Blondie (and a myriad of lesser bands) by the decade's end. These bands represented New York punk to the world.

In Britain, the punk scene was much larger and more overtly political, even if that politics was often nihilistic in nature (think

Sex Pistols). Unlike most punk groups in the US, punk bands sold enough records to actually make the charts in Britain. The music was often classified together with New Wave and reggae music by mainstream critics and observers. On the west coast of the United States, the primary urban areas hosting some kind of punk scene were San Francisco, Los Angeles and Vancouver, British Columbia. In San Francisco, the scene originally centered around the Mabuhay Gardens club in San Francisco's North Beach district. The Dead Kennedys did the most to make this venue famous. Eventually, the all-ages club run by Berkeley's Gilman Street Music Collective would make a longer lasting name in the punk world. Los Angeles was home to punk bands like X and Black Flag (actually from suburban Orange County). The latter group was an originator of what became known as hardcore, a fast-paced, loud and minimalist form of punk rock. The Canadian city of Vancouver, BC featured hardcore punk as well, most notably the band DOA. Already a city with a prominent counterculture community in its Gastown District, Vancouver was also home to a militant leftist and anarchist community. Those radical politics would come to define much of Vancouver's punk scene. Punk music and the accompanying subculture would truly take off in the 1980s, a fitting rebuke to the harsh reality of Ronald Reagan and Maggie Thatcher's class hatred.

D.O.A.'s Political Punk

In 1978 Vancouver left / anarchist Joey Shithead (guitar/vocals) left the band Black Skull and formed D.O.A with Chuck Biscuits on drums and Randy Rampage on bass and vocals. Their politics and brash musical stylings ticked off members of their audience and provoked fights. Their slogan was "Talk minus Action equals Zero." The fights would bring the police, who would wade into the crowds both in and outside of the clubs they played, creating greater melees. As their reputation for trouble grew, it became more difficult for them to play clubs interested only in the profits punk bands were beginning to bring by the late 1970s. Despite this, DOA found plenty of sympathetic folks and organizations to play for, their politically charged music striking a chord in the hearts of some Reagan era youth.

Chapter 2

Test Me Test Me,
Why Don't You Arrest Me?

Because of the illegal nature of their lifestyle (drugs and otherwise) and the punitive attempts by police and other authorities to shut that lifestyle down, many young people in the 1960s and 1970s had seen the inside of a jail by the time they were in their twenties. It seems safe to state that the percentage of those in the Sixties generation who had been arrested was considerably higher than that of their parents' generation, especially in the white community. Perhaps it was this fact that created a sympathy (if not outright empathy) for those black and brown Americans who were imprisoned. Whatever the reason, by the early 1970s, there was a substantial prisoner rights and support movement comprised of members of the New Left and the counterculture. This movement grew in proportion to the increased repression instituted under the Nixon regime. Examples of this support included benefit concerts featuring rock bands in the San Francisco area for those arrested during the May 1969 People's Park riots and other benefits for members of the Black Panthers facing prison or already in jail.

The trial of the Soledad Brothers in Marin County, California and the attempt to free them multiplied the prisoner support movement exponentially. The men on trial were charged with killing a guard at Soledad prison in California's Central Valley. The defenders of the accused claimed that the authorities really had no idea who the guard's killers were, but had charged the men known as the Soledad Brothers because of their political activism and leadership roles in the prisoner rights movement. George Jackson was the best known of the defendants. A Black Panther, his book about his life titled *Soledad Brother: The Prison Letters of George Jackson* became an international bestseller and his name was synonymous with revolution. George Jackson's younger brother Jonathan was deeply involved in the movement to free the Soledad Brothers.

The younger Jackson's frustration with the legal process grew as hopes for George's freedom dimmed. Finally, on August 7, 1970,

Jonathan Jackson stood up during a session of the Soledad Brothers trial, pulled out a shotgun, distributed weapons to the defendants and took several hostages, including the judge. This group then took a van and attempted to leave the courthouse building. They never made it. Most of the passengers in the van died in a hail of gunfire from police and corrections officers' weapons. Controversial university professor, prisoner rights advocate, Communist party member and Black Panther sympathizer Angela Davis was arrested soon after the incident. Davis was charged with "aggravated kidnapping and first degree murder" because she had supposedly bought some of the guns used in the incident. In addition, she was friends with both Jackson brothers, had written letters to George Jackson, visited him in prison and been very active in the campaign to free the Soledad Brothers. She and George were romantically linked.

Angela went underground and remained on the run until October 13, 1970, when she was finally arrested by the FBI. During her time on the run, she was placed on the FBI's Ten Most Wanted list. This only enhanced her status among antiestablishment youth around the world. Her trial and the campaign to free her became an international struggle, bringing together musicians (the Rolling Stones wrote the song "Sweet Black Angel" and John Lennon and Yoko Ono wrote "Angela" about the case), leftists of virtually every sect, Black nationalists, counterculture freaks and several governments. After a trial watched intently by the world, she was acquitted of all charges in June 1972.

The Symbionese Liberation Army (or SLA), was a second generation urban guerrilla group. Its brand of armed struggle was inspired by that of the Weather Underground Organization (WUO), which had arisen from the self-ignited ashes of the Students for a Democratic Society (SDS). The demise of SDS, owing to an insistence on revolutionary purity among its various factions and a fair dose of government provocateurism, harassment and surveillance, had left a vacuum in the political activities of the counterculture. Although the Yippies remained a source of theatrical activism, the group's strength was never in organizing a lasting movement. After the political conventions of 1972, which saw Yippie non-leaders Abbie Hoffman and Jerry Rubin being called out by a group known as the Zippies for not being radical enough, the only issue the Yippies could turn any numbers out nationally for was related to their campaign to legalize marijuana. There was also a turn by more serious leftists away from trying to organize the counterculture and towards studying various strains of Marxism-Leninism. This turn towards more traditional communism, which resulted in what became known as the new communist movement, combined with the McGovern campaign for president that organized primarily around ending the war in Vietnam, had pushed most of the counterculture element of the New Left away from communism/socialism and into the arms of the Democratic Party. The influx of former new leftists into the Democrats' arms would make the 1972 convention one of the most open and progressive mainstream political conventions in US history. It would also create a backlash from the party's more conservative and pro-military/big business wing. The leaders of this backlash reformulated party rules and processes in order to take the party back from the leftist upstarts. By changing the party rules, the traditional wing of the Democratic Party ensured that a convention like 1972 and a candidate like George McGovern would never again have a real chance to win the Democratic nomination.

On the other hand, the new leftist political radicals who were joining the new communist groups continued to organize in the workplace and on campus. To fit into the factory culture as they perceived it, some of these groups decided that members should cut their hair, end their alternative living arrangements and, in extreme cases, turn off their rock and roll. As it turned out, this trend towards conservatism in the radicals' social trappings was based on an incorrect understanding of the US working class and, for those not willing to amend their analysis to the new nature of that class, would determine the increasing irrelevance of many of the groups in the new communist movement. Contrary to these groups' analysis, by the mid-1970s, the US working class was not primarily middle-aged white and male. Instead, workers were increasingly female, young and non-white. As for the white men entering the work force, they were also considerably less conservative than their predecessors. Even if they had never been to an antiwar protest or dropped LSD, chances were that younger US workers listened to rock music and at least knew people who smoked pot. That in itself made them considerably different than their fathers.

The SLA ignored all of this. Like their WUO compatriots, they lived in a different world. In part, this was due to their residence in the San Francisco Bay Area—where the Sixties were still very much alive, especially when compared to the rest of the United States. Although there were still plenty of freaks to be found in many college towns, the few remaining hippie ghettos in big cities, and in communes around the country, the retreat of the Sixties counterculture was obvious to those who had populated those same communities only a few years earlier. The combination of police harassment and gentrification was doing its part to facilitate the retreat of the youth oriented, leisure based counterculture. Only in places where the counterculture had been able to build strong institutions was it able to resist the forces arrayed against its permanence. It was this reason, then, that the counterculture was still a dominant force in Berkeley and San Francisco. Despite their often incoherent politics (or maybe because of them), the SLA were able to gain enough support in the Bay Area to keep themselves shielded from the police. In part, this was because they looked like most other people their age and blended into the local environs.

The SLA had its roots in a prisoner literacy group located at California's Vacaville Prison. College students from the San Francisco Area working with prison officials organized a group designed to teach prisoners how to read and write. One of the prisoners in this particular group, named Donald DeFreeze, became friends with many members of the group and adopted (at least in word) their political philosophy. After escaping from Vacaville through the prison laundry, DeFreeze joined up with the students and helped form the Symbionese Liberation Army. In 1972, two members of the group killed Oakland Schools superintendent Marcus Foster, a Black man, because he wanted to institute a student ID-card system in the schools. This murder alienated much of the Bay Area Left, who saw Foster as a mostly-progressive individual, from the group. Some folks on the Left, including the Black Panthers, instituted an investigation of the SLA's members and discovered that DeFreeze, who was now calling himself Cinque (after the leader of the Amistad slave ship rebellion) had links to an undercover unit of the California Highway Patrol and the Los Angeles Police Department. There was speculation that the literacy group itself had been set-up by authorities to spy on and entrap young radicals. Two other SLA members, Bill and Emily Harris, also had backgrounds that appeared suspicious to the Panthers and their team of investigators. If the actions of the SLA were not enough to drive potentially sympathetic people away from the group, these suspicions convinced the Panthers and many others on the Left to disavow any connection with the SLA.

On February 4, 1974 the SLA kidnapped newspaper heiress and college student Patty Hearst from the Berkeley apartment she shared with her boyfriend Stephen Weed. The original demand of the SLA involved trading Hearst for some SLA members already in prison for killing the Oakland Schools Superintendent. When this demand was rejected, the SLA demanded Patty's family distribute seventy dollars worth of food to every poor California family. The family responded by immediately distributing $6 million to people in poor neighborhoods of Oakland and other California cities. Afterwards, the SLA refused to release Patty because the family had not distributed enough food and the food that was distributed was found to be of poor quality. By April, Patty Hearst had allegedly joined the SLA, renamed herself Tania (after Che Guevara's companion), and was photographed carrying an M1 carbine during a bank holdup. The authorities ramped up the search for the SLA as the group carried out a series of dramatic robberies in California. On May 17, 1974 the Los Angeles police and members of the California Highway Patrol laid siege to a house in Compton, California (near the Watts section of Los Angeles) rented by SLA members. After several hours during which the house was set on fire by the police, the siege ended and the six SLA members inside were all dead. Hearst and other members were not in the house. On September 18, 1975, Patty and another member Wendy Yoshimura were captured in San Francisco. Only two SLA members remained underground. They would not be captured for decades.

The saga of the SLA turned out to be, more than anything else, a media event. Even after the siege and deaths in Compton, which many stations televised live, the press remained interested. As an indication of the alienation from law enforcement and the State still felt by the counterculture, it is important to note that the remaining SLA members were able to stay on the run for as long as they did because they were assisted by some counterculture communities and individuals. These allegedly included the leftist athlete and counterculture sports guru Bill Scott, his wife Micki and possibly even basketball player Bill Walton. Like Scott, Walton was well-known for his leftist political views and his participation in the counterculture life. The authorities were unable to get those who helped the SLA members remain underground to talk.

Native Americans

Merry Prankster and Whole Earth Catalog editor Stewart Brand organized a performance piece in the 1960s he called America Needs Indians. Later in the decade (and into the 1970s), Native Americans began a series of political actions designed to force the US government to honor its treaties with various Indian nations. These actions included the occupation of Alcatraz Island near San Francisco, several protests in Minnesota and the Dakotas, a multi-week occupation of the Bureau of Indian Affairs offices in Washington, DC in 1972, and a months-long 1973 faceoff with federal troops, FBI agents and US marshals in Pine Ridge, South Dakota. All of these actions were organized under the auspices of the American Indian Movement (AIM), a group of radical Native Americans representing various nations across the United States. Support for the group came from across the radical Left and the counterculture.

As the 1970s continued, Native Americans continued to organize protest encampments and lobbying efforts. Two of the better known organizing efforts revolved around land issues and the mining of resources from Native American lands: specifically in the Four Corners area of the US Southwest in an area called Big Mountain and in the Black Hills region of the Dakotas. Gatherings at these two sites were well-attended by Native Americans, freaks and various political organizations. Although there were quarrels between some freaks and the organizers over the use of mood-modifying substances which the Native Americans forbade in part because of the ravages alcohol created in the native American community and because the organizers did not want to give the police an excuse to bust the gatherings, for the most part the gatherings came off smoothly and cemented relationships between Native American groups and some counterculture organizations wanting to provide material support.

In 1978, AIM organized a march across North America. Called The Longest Walk, its intent was to prevent the passing of a Congressional Bill abrogating all US treaties with Native American tribes and nations. The walk began at the American Indian Center in East Oakland, California. The sendoff was attended by members of the Communist party, USA, the Revolutionary Communist Party, several dozen Native Americans who lived in the Bay Area, individual hippies and the Hog Farm. After walking 3200 miles, several thousand walkers (Native Americans and their supporters) arrived in Washington, DC for a protest against the proposed legislation. Congress did not pass the bill and it did not become law.

The last major protests against the US war in Southeast Asia began in late April of 1971. These ten days of protest were actually several separately organized actions designed to make opposition to the war impossible for Congress and the White House to avoid. In addition, the more radical organizers planned to make Washington, DC itself ungovernable. To clarify their intention, these groups, led by a loose-knit confederation of political and counterculture individuals calling themselves the Mayday Tribe, created the slogan, "If the government won't stop the war, then the people will stop the government." The protests the Mayday Tribe organized incorporated anti-imperialist politics, rock and roll, and serious direct action tactics. The direct actions that occurred on May 1 and May 2, 1971 were preceded by a week of more traditional protests that included lobbying of Congress and numerous rallies sponsored by a coalition calling themselves the People's Coalition for Peace and Justice (PCPJ). This latter group included antiwar members of Congress, clergy from numerous faiths (many who had been active in the antiwar movement for years), the Socialist Workers Party, and numerous pacifist organizations. In addition, the Vietnam Veterans Against the War were camped on the National Mall carrying out a protest action they called Operation Dewey Canyon II. The Nixon administration had refused to grant camping permits to the VVAW and threatened to have them removed by force. However, fearing a media and popular backlash to an operation reminiscent of General McArthur's routing of the Bonus Army's Washington, DC encampment back in 1932, Nixon's Justice Department backed down and allowed the veterans to remain on the Mall. As for the PCPJ, one of their rallies on the Capitol Steps was attacked by police. Hundreds of protesters were swept up in this raid and thrown in detention centers, including the RFK Stadium in southeast DC. Some congresspeople and other government officials were also snared by the sweeps.

However, the biggest and most dramatic protests of the ten-day-period began on Saturday, May 1st. Approximately forty thousand protesters gathered in Washington's West Potomac Park to listen to rock bands, speakers and other performers. After the concert, which went into the night, most of the protesters camped in the park. Those protesters who had organized affinity groups prepared for the demonstrations set to begin the following Monday when Washington went back to work. During the concert, military and police helicopters buzzed the area, but stopped when some groups of protesters began releasing helium filled balloons. The pilots were afraid the balloons and the attached strings would get caught in the helicopter rotor blades. Meanwhile, the Justice Department cancelled the permits for the campsite and any future protests, clearing the way for a police raid of the encampment the morning of Sunday, May 2, 1971. This was a blatant attempt by the authorities to prevent the massive direct actions planned for Monday. After the raids, about half of the protesters scrambled out of town. The remainder found shelter in churches, colleges and other friendly sites in the area. The direct action protests would go forward.

The next day around dawn, Monday, thousands of protesters flooded the streets of Washington, DC. Their tentative plan was to prevent government workers from getting to their job sites, especially at those buildings connected to the military and the Justice Department. People blocked streets with their bodies, with hastily constructed barricades, with broken down cars, and with trash cans and trash. Several thousand played cat-and-mouse with the police, blocking streets then running away when the police came. The police, armored in full riot gear, attacked the protesters and arrested as many as they could. By the following day, over 12,000 protesters had been arrested, many of them illegally and without cause. Martial law had come to Washington, DC for the second time in five years (the previous crackdown was during the rebellion after the murder of Dr. Martin Luther King, Jr.)

As noted earlier, this was the last big antiwar protest of the Vietnam era. It was also the last antiwar protest that included the conscious organization of hippies and freaks. The war would continue for four more years, but the will to fight against it on the streets of America had evaporated. Nixon realized that young American men would no longer fight the war and he pushed his Vietnamization program with even greater earnest. This program not only involved the removal of US troops from Vietnam and placing the bulk of the fighting responsibility on troops from the Saigon military, it also involved the bombing of Laos and Cambodia. This proved to be a cynical, murderous transfer of pointless death and killing.

Several lawsuits were filed against the Justice Department and other law enforcement institutions in the wake of the mass arrests at the Mayday protests. Years later, and after thousands of hours of work by attorneys and others, several hundred of those who were detained received checks from the government for damages they incurred. A friend of mine who was arrested at a PCPJ rally on the Capitol steps received $7000.00. He had spent two days in RFK stadium and been beaten by the police during his arrest. Once inside the stadium, antiwar medics patched him up.

On August 28, 1973 Abbie Hoffman was arrested for conspiracy to distribute cocaine. According to biographer (and fellow traveler) Jonah Raskin, Hoffman had been involved in smuggling and dealing cocaine for at least three years. Abbie insisted until his death in 1989 that he was the victim of entrapment. However, in drug-related cases, the line between entrapment and what would constitute a reasonable search is very fine indeed. By 1974, the dismemberment of the Fourth Amendment (against unreasonable search and seizure) to the US Constitution was already well underway. Although there will always remain some question as to whether or not Abbie was set up, the fact was that he was busted and faced fifteen years to life in prison. Instead of going to prison, Hoffman went on the lam and would not resurface until 1980 as Barry Freed, environmental activist. During his period underground, Yippies in different cities hosted many benefit concerts for Abbie. At these benefits attendees were encouraged to wear costumes. It was rumored that this was so that Abbie could come to the concerts if he chose. Indeed, my friends and I remain convinced we saw him at one of these shows in Washington, DC. After Hoffman turned himself in, he served a four-month sentence and then spent some time in a halfway house.

Another activist, Scott Camil, perhaps as well known in his home state of Florida and among Vietnam Veterans Against the War (VVAW) circles as Hoffman was nationally, was also involved in a cocaine bust involving a probable frame-up. He was not as fortunate as Hoffman (not to say Hoffman's luck was good). In fact, he was shot in the back by a DEA agent during a 1974 cocaine deal as he attempted to leave the agent's car. Camil survived the shooting. Since he survived, the DEA charged him with possession with intent to distribute. Camil claimed that an unidentified hitchhiker had left the cocaine with him; the police allowed the hitchhiker to leave the car within minutes after Camil was shot. The implication being that the cocaine had been planted.

Scott Camil was a key organizer for the VVAW. He had spent 20 months in Vietnam as a Marine and when he came back he joined the organization. By 1971, he was on President Nixon's enemies list (so was Hoffman, along with hundreds of other US citizens) and was characterized by FBI director J. Edgar Hoover as an "individual whose activities must be neutralized at earliest possible time." Camil and seven other VVAW members of the Gainesville, Florida chapter were charged with conspiracy to disrupt the 1972 Republican National Convention in Miami, Florida. The convention was moved to Miami after law enforcement determined that the original host city San Diego was too dangerous. As it turned out, Camil's defense team was able to prove that the Gainesville VVAW chapter had been infiltrated by an FBI informant and the supposed conspiracy existed only in the minds of the Bureau. The Gainesville Eight, as they became known, were all acquitted. The drug related frame-up and subsequent shooting of Camil proved to his supporters that the government had not given up its desire to "neutralize" him. By using the DEA to arrest him instead of the FBI, the authorities thought they might be able to get a conviction despite the obvious entrapment involved. Furthermore, the drug arrest might discredit him in the minds of those supporters unwilling to be associated with the sale of illegal drugs.

As Camil's and Hoffman's experiences prove, the confluence of the counterculture and politics made the possibility of drug arrests all too real. Furthermore, unless one accepted the counterculture's perception that drug arrests were actually political in nature because of governmental repression of the counterculture, it was easier to portray those charged as plain criminals. The Black Liberation movement had confronted this scenario for years and warned white activists to keep their substance use out of the public eye for security reasons. This was but one reason why much of the straight Left in the 1970s showed little tolerance for drug use among its members. Conversely, that intolerance pushed many politically active freaks who smoked pot away from those groups.

The War is Over

April 30, 1975. The war was over. Really over. This wasn't like the peace treaty all the leaders signed in 1973 that didn't really end anything. No, this time it was over. The television in the University of Maryland Student Union showed video footage of helicopters leaving the U.S. embassy roof with a few remaining GIs and other Americans inside while Vietnamese hung on to the sides. Meanwhile the Vietnamese whose side had won were celebrating the entry of NLF and Hanoi forces into Saigon, which was now Ho Chi Minh City.

My friends and I were exhilarated. A war we had known most of our lives was over. A war which seemed an adventure when I was a young boy playing Little League baseball and war games and had become a source of fear and anger as I grew older. A war which took friends of mine and killed some, made others killers and zombies, and forced all of us to grow up before we were ready. A war which took my father away from my family for over a year and had us wondering every day whether he would come back. And had me wondering if my brothers and I would have to go also. A war which showed Americans what America was really about. An America which wasn't pretty, or even honorable. A war which I had begun opposing as a 13-year old by flashing a peace sign and singing "Give Peace a Chance" while my dad was in Danang, and ended up celebrating the victory of America's enemy.

The night of the Vietnamese victory, Pat M. and I invited ourselves to a Student Association-sponsored banquet at the University of Maryland. Pat was a friend and reasonably well-known on campus as a rabble rouser. He had recently begun attending meetings of the radical group I was associated with--the Revolutionary Student Brigades. Once he and I realized we shared a fondness for pot and a passionate dislike of the system, we began to spend lots of time stirring things up. As for this particular dinner, the food was good, but the wine was better. We lifted a half dozen bottles during the post dinner speeches and headed out to the streets to celebrate. On our way to Route 1 and the strip of bars there we stopped at a friend's dorm room and drew up a banner reading, "Long Live the People of Vietnam", and scored a couple tabs of acid and a corkscrew. After all, this antiwar movement was about more than Washington's war against the Vietnamese. It was a war of its own against the consciousness that started the war in the first place. John Foster Dulles, Richard Nixon, LBJ. The fear of communism, sexuality and marijuana. Many of us against Washington's war for empire were fighting another war to make our world a place where fear took a backseat to joy.

By the time we made it to the street the acid was edging out the fog of the alcohol and providing a nice clarity to the night. Pat and I opened a bottle of wine each, spread out our banner, and shouted some revolutionary slogans about Ho Chi Minh and so on. After a half hour or so, another thirty people had joined us. By then we were spilling into the streets, drinking wine and smoking weed. Of course, the police showed up.

The funny thing was, they didn't do much. After asking us what was going on, they told us to stay out of the road and drove off. I'm still not sure what Pat and I told them but, whatever it was, it worked. In retrospect, I put it among those moments where the clarity of psychedelic thought patterns befuddles the linear thinker, the authoritarian, so much that they just don't want to bother with figuring it out. So, instead, they left it alone and hoped we would just go away. Later, we headed into DC to celebrate with a few hundred other antiwarriors.

A couple weeks later, Gerald Ford ordered an attack on Cambodia after the merchant ship Mayaguez was seized and released. A final flurry of killing from a vanquished nation.

Chapter 3

Celebrating Independence?

1976 was the 200th anniversary of the signing of the US Declaration of Independence. This meant the people of the United States (and the world) would be subjected to a year of US jingoism and lies about freedom, the rights of the individual, and the natural superiority of the US system of government. The opposition to the festivities included the Yippies and their now annual Smoke-In, protests sponsored by various new communist groups and one by a liberal network organized by populist progressive and environmentalist Jeremy Rifkin. The group he chaired, the Peoples Bicentennial Commission (PBC), would share the National Mall in Washington DC with the official celebration on July 4th. Johnny Cash and the Beach Boys were featured at the official celebration, while the PBC's rally and concert occupied the other end of the Mall near the Capitol. In Philadelphia, home of the Liberty Bell and the city where the Declaration of Independence was signed, the Revolutionary Communist Party and other Marxist-Leninist groups marched to their own drums through different working class neighborhoods. The Yippies' protest blended with the People's Bicentennial rally while maintaining an ideological distance. Rumors persisted that the Grateful Dead would be performing for free. They did not. There was a severe shortage of good weed at the Yippie Smoke-In and no psychedelics to be found.

The shortage of psychedelics had been the case since the arrests of many acid chemists and the demise of the Brotherhood of Eternal Love's distribution network earlier in the decade. The Brotherhood of Eternal Love was the stuff of counterculture legend. Operating out of the Laguna Beach, California freak and surfer community, the Brotherhood began their mission of spreading peace, love and LSD by smuggling topnotch hashish from Nepal. Once they had made enough money hauling dope, they hired a couple chemists already familiar with LSD manufacture, including Owsley Stanley apprentices Nick Sands and Tim Scully. They also invited Timothy Leary to join the group, which he did. Leary and the chemists shared the Brotherhood's goal to turn on the world. The LSD brand they created, called Orange Sunshine, was manufactured and distributed via a very loose confederation of dealers and freaks across North America. It was even occasionally found in Europe, especially on or near US military bases. One assumes GIs were the main people distributing the drug in Europe.

The Brotherhood manufactured and distributed millions of hits. They were occasionally passed out for free at Grateful Dead concerts and rock festivals. A friend of mine who attended the April 1971 Dead concerts at the Fillmore East told me stories of Orange Sunshine wrapped in balls of foil thrown out into the audience by people on the stage. *The Village Voice* published a wonderful piece in the spring of 1971 about an Orange Sunshine manufacturer/distributor who went by the name of Sunshine John. It seems John was somehow connected to the Brotherhood and, as part of its mission to spread Orange Sunshine around the world, became one of its primary distributors on the US east coast.[ix]

Naturally, all that LSD drew the attention of the authorities. Until the early 1970s, most of the anti-narcotics work concerning the Brotherhood was carried out by local police in Laguna Beach. One officer in particular, Nicholas Purcell, was behind most of the arrests and harassment of the Brotherhood and those who distributed its acid and hashish. When the war on drugs intensified under Richard Nixon's White House, Purcell and his cohorts were able to involve California and federal agencies in their mission to destroy the Brotherhood.

Meanwhile, the Brotherhood continued to smuggle marijuana products and distribute LSD. Simultaneously, many of them were moving to Maui, Hawaii after their ranch in the canyons was raided. Timothy Leary was arrested and Brotherhood leader/founder John Griggs overdosed on synthetic psylocibin. In addition, the mission to spread peace and love via LSD was foundering. Like so many other spiritually-inclined endeavors, when the Brotherhood lost it spiritual leader, the mission became confused by the more earthly desires of some of those next in line.

The distribution network collapsed when Brotherhood members were busted in Hawaii, California and Oregon on October 5, 1972. Other counterculture chemists, such as the aforementioned Augustus Bear Owsley, were already serving time. Their removal from the scene, and an increasing fascination with cocaine and a rather dismaying increase in the availability of the animal tranquilizer PCP (which lived up to its reputation in middle class America's fantasy as a drug to be feared) only made the counterculture drug scene more dangerous and depressing. LSD would not appear in a similar abundance until 1977 or later, depending on one's location. Writing from personal experience, LSD was much easier to find at music festivals beginning in the summer of 1977 than it had been since 1973. Mostly available in blotter form, the quality was comparable to that found earlier in the decade.[x]

The Yippies continued to organize Smoke-Ins and marches dedicated to getting marijuana legalized, opposing racism and spreading their version of the freak counterculture. One such Smoke-In took place each Fourth of July weekend in Washington, DC. The crowds never grew larger than a couple thousand and included mostly young people from up and down the east coast of the United States. Predominantly long-haired and white-skinned, by the late 1970s, the bands that played were mostly punk rockers from New York City and the DC area. In 1977, I spent a couple afternoons the week prior to the Fourth of July weekend at a Yippie household in northwest Washington, DC helping a dozen other people roll a couple pounds of donated red Colombian marijuana into joints made from American flag rolling papers. When we were done, there were literally thousands of joints. The afternoon of July 4th, 1977 Yippies began passing out the joints to the crowd that had walked from the Mall where the Smoke-In's music stage was located to Lafayette Park across from the White House. Soon, hundreds of people were smoking pot in a national park surrounded by Park Police on horses. When the cops began making arrests, I moved out. The music on the National Mall continued long into the night until police finally cleared the area.

Timothy Leary, whom Richard Nixon once labeled the most dangerous man in America, was a member of the Brotherhood of Eternal Love. After his arrest and conviction for possessing two marijuana roaches (the butts of a joint), Leary was sentenced (after years of wrangling in court) to twenty years in prison on January 21, 1970. Although the bust was almost certainly a frame-up and the sentence was overkill, the long-festering desire of the authorities to lock him up overrode any constitutional concerns. This would become the standard operating procedure in the burgeoning war on drugs. The Bill of Rights was rapidly losing whatever meaning it had as Nixon stepped up his war on the Black Liberation movement, the counterculture and the New Left, much of it under the guise of a war on drugs. The idea of civil liberties in America would never be the same. On September 13, 1970, the Weather Underground broke Leary out of prison. The Brotherhood of Eternal Love had paid 25,000 dollars to what Leary called "a crack team" of revolutionaries to break their man out of the San Luis Obispo Correctional Facility. Within days, Leary and his wife Rosemary were in Algeria as guests of the exiled Black Panther leader Eldridge Cleaver. Some in the counterculture who still believed the revolution might be coming hoped this act would signal the beginning of an alliance between the political and countercultural underground, with the potential of moving the revolution further. However, Leary's stay at the Panther compound in Algeria would be brief.

Leary's lazy approach to security issues and his continued drug use proved too much for the Panthers guarding the compound. After just a few weeks Leary was asked to leave. In 1971, he and his wife did so. They spent a short time in Switzerland, where Leary was arrested by Swiss police at the request of US authorities. However, the Swiss government refused to extradite him back to the United States. Rosemary left Leary later that year. Eventually, Leary ended up in Afghanistan with another woman, Joanna Harcourt-Smith, a socialite who was rumored to be working with the Drug Enforcement Agency and perhaps Interpol to capture Leary. He was arrested in Kabul in 1973 and brought back to the US, where he talked his way out of a long prison sentence. Rumors swirled through counterculture and New Left circles that Leary had ratted out several key figures in the Weather Underground and the Brotherhood of Eternal Love to authorities. Some of Leary's friends defended him, even publishing a letter stating their belief that Leary did not turn in anybody and that the rumors suggesting he had been an informer were circulated by the authorities, who wanted to hang a snitch jacket on the good doctor. Most people seemed to believe that the information Leary provided (if any) was old news and incriminated no one. Indeed, the WUO remained a secure organization for a few more years and no one was busted in the group based on anything Leary might have said. However, in a lengthy *High Times* interview with Attorney Michael Kennedy, once one of Leary's lawyers, Kennedy called Leary one of the "most opportunistic and unscrupulous scoundrels" he had ever known. Kennedy also disagreed with those who believed that Leary had given Federal agents nothing of value. He thought Leary had definitely informed on various people, but admitted he did not know for sure. He further stated that Leary's ability to charm continued to amaze even a hard-to-con attorney like Kennedy himself.[xii]

In 1974, the cost of a baggie of marijuana in the Washington, DC/Baltimore area ran around twenty five dollars, when it could be found. Usually, the weed came from some place in Mexico. It was often green and heavy with stems and seeds. Occasionally, more exotic strains showed up at one's dealer. Some of the later included strains from the Mexican states of Michoacan, Oaxaca, and the grail of them all, Acapulco Gold. These strains were slightly more expensive and smokers gladly paid the extra cash since the quality was exponentially better. In addition, the higher quality weed was often sold by weight to the individual consumer, whereas the less expensive stuff was measured by sight. For example, one bought a lid of pot that might measure five fingers high in the bag, measured by holding one's extended fingers up to the baggie. This bag might weigh an ounce or a few grams more or less. Of course, prices and obtainability varied by locale. However, because most marijuana was imported at the time, the market also depended on border enforcement and other factors that had nothing to do with domestic growing. When there was a lack of weed coming across the border in the 1970s, it affected the price across the whole country. At the time, most domestically grown pot was very low in THC content (the mood modifying molecule in marijuana) and did not usually keep one high for very long, if it got one high at all. Consequently, this homegrown had little value as a recreational drug.

Despite a growing consensus that pot should be legal, law enforcement did not stop arresting people. Thousands of marijuana smokers went to prison every year. Numbers for all drug-related arrests climbed even higher after Richard Nixon declared his "war on drugs" in 1971. By mid-decade, about half-a-million people were being arrested each year for marijuana possession. What these numbers suggest is that, despite government efforts to reduce drug use, more people were getting high than ever before. Some states and municipalities responded by decriminalizing the possession of small amounts of weed. Others did the opposite. The federal government continued to oppose any attempts to decriminalize or legalize marijuana.

Into this fraught scenario came *High Times* magazine. Not only did this magazine list approximate street prices of marijuana and other drugs, it featured articles on the history of drugs, legal questions concerning drug use, drug enforcement news, and features about politics, music, communal living, street life and other aspects of the counterculture. Occasionally, the writers were well-known authors and figures from both the mainstream and counterculture. William Burroughs, Jerry Rubin, Hunter S. Thompson, Charles Bukowski and Truman Capote all wrote for the magazine.

High Times was founded by drug smuggler and Yippie activist Tom Forcade. Forcade's journey to becoming the publisher of a national magazine for the counterculture-cum-drug culture started like many other male members of his generation. He joined the military to avoid the draft and then got discharged after being declared unfit for military service. Then Forcade tried the so-called straight world by working toward a business degree. After dropping out of college he joined a commune in Tucson, Arizona that ended up being raided by the police. The bust increased his paranoia and his desire to live outside the mainstream. After a few months of vagabonding and publishing a small circulation underground paper called *Orpheus*, he drove to New York and, with the *East Village Other*'s John Wilcock, started the Underground Press Syndicate (UPS). This clearinghouse for underground newspapers around the country eventually counted over three hundred papers in its network and, with the Liberation News Service (LNS), the two operations included virtually every underground media outlet in the United States, plus many outlets located overseas.

Like other personalities in the counterculture, Forcade had his detractors. Rumors of police infiltration and even covert funding of the UPS flourished for a time but were never substantiated (probably because they were false.) As a Yippie, Forcade challenged the group's non-leaders Abbie Hoffman and Jerry Rubin in 1972 because of their support for antiwar Democratic candidate George McGovern and insisted that the Yippies not back away from protests planned against the GOP convention in Miami that year. After a series of disagreements that were most likely exacerbated by police provocateurs, he and other (mostly) younger Yippies formed their own loose-knit organization they called the Zippies. The Zippies then took over much of the organization of the 1972 Miami protests. Once again, some folks in the street spread rumors that Forcade was an agent provocateur. There was never any proof of these charges, which likely stemmed from petty sniping by others jealous of his success or rumors begun by real provocateurs hoping to discredit him. There were also those on the side of the law who had made it their purpose to put Forcade away. True to his outlaw persona, though, this only made Forcade more careful and more determined to spread the gospel of the counterculture as he saw it. By 1974, he had assembled the funding and staff to begin the project he would be forever identified with: *High Times* magazine.

High Times' publishing genius derived from focusing on the aspect of the counterculture that remains to this day--the use of mind altering drugs other than alcohol--the magazine weaved reportage on drug busts, drug production, music and politics together in a bowl full of information that was instructive, entertaining and relevant to the lives and lifestyles of a good number of long term and newly aware counterculture freaks. It was as if Gilbert Shelton's comix characters the Furry Freak Brothers had special-ordered a magazine just for their stoned reading pleasure. Yet, *High Times* proved to be much more than just a hippie rag. When the punk subculture began to insinuate itself into the Lower Manhattan street scene, Forcade recognized its antiestablishment foundation and helped get the magazine *Punk* off the ground. Unlike a lot of counterculture hippies, Forcade understood the dismay the punks expressed toward the Sixties counterculture and did not take personally any insults or mockery thrown his way from that quarter. Like his more proletarian counterparts publishing *Yipster Times* on Bleecker Street, this was due in part to Forcade's closeness to the street, which was rapidly turning into punk turf. Yippies on the other side of the North American continent, notably Vancouver's Ken Lester and David Spaner, championed the punk scene. In fact, they were the managers of Canada's two most notorious political punk bands, D.O.A. and The Subhumans.

Besides sharing a similar understanding of the punk movement, Forcade helped finance the *Yipster Times/Overthrow* magazine until his death. *High Times* magazine, which began as a mimeographed sheet, became a glossy journal recognized by journalists, policymakers and others well beyond its original audience. Forcade committed suicide in 1978. The magazine continued after his death, but its editorial policy changed, as did the drugs it championed. Like the culture it described, powdered drugs like cocaine and even heroin began to fill its pages at a volume never seen while Forcade was alive.

Despite the focus on mostly illegal substances, the magazine was much more than a journal about drugs while under Forcade's direction. The staff writers approached the counterculture from a multitude of favorable viewpoints and covered virtually every aspect of it with a depth not found in any other journal with a comparable circulation. This coverage usually focused on politics, drugs and the exploits of the State. Most issues featured an interview. A small sampling of issues includes interviews with attorney Michael Kennedy, members of the Weather Underground, LSD manufacturer Nick Sands, Hunter S. Thompson, and John Lydon of the Sex Pistols. Another issue featured a conversation between Yippies Abbie Hoffman and Jerry Rubin while Abbie was underground. Article topics in the magazine included histories of human interactions with various drugs throughout history.

Other essays charted the birth and development of the Sixties counterculture, the fascist tendencies of Walt Disney, and Rastafarianism. *High Times* was the only national journal that took the counterculture in all its manifestations seriously in the 1970s. By decade's end, it was also the only national journal still around that accepted the consciousness and ethos that inspired and informed the freak culture. *Rolling Stone* may have covered the music scene, but it never accepted the extreme political and cultural wings of the counterculture that High Times ultimately championed.

The Cesspool called Watergate

Underlying the national situation in the United States from 1973 through 1975 was the criminal and political "cesspool called Watergate," as Gil Scott Heron famously put it in his song "H2Ogate Blues." Probably the political crime of the century in the US, its revelations exposed a pit of corruption and criminality that only served to confirm the cynicism permeating the counterculture and the fears of its more political elements. To be honest, it also stirred up a bit of joy among those who had always hated Richard Nixon and the culture he represented. One of the first Impeach Nixon rallies occurred in Manhattan's Union Square in October 1973. Phil Ochs sang his remade "Here's to the State of Richard Nixon" and approximately three thousand participants listened and sang along. There would be more rallies around the nation, with the biggest one taking place in April 1974 on the National Mall. Close to 80,000 people attended this rally and listened to speeches. Near the end of the rally, a couple thousand protesters ran from the rally site towards the Justice Department building. A skirmish between police and protesters took place, with rocks and tear gas thrown. The lackluster nature of the Impeach Nixon movement among the American people--as measured by the relatively few rallies and attendance at those rallies—indicates an apathy and cynicism prevalent among the young by 1974 but also perhaps a belief that the system might actually provide justice. As it turned out, Nixon resigned the presidency and got away with multiple crimes.

The resignation took place August 9, 1974 and was televised to the world. The three major news outlets had set up their equipment in Lafayette Park across from the White House in the morning before the speech. People began gathering while the media set up. Tourists, journalists, locals, Yippies and other political freaks, and curious teens filled the park by mid-afternoon. There was a party atmosphere. Some people were drinking discreetly from bottles wrapped in brown paper bags and some brave souls were even smoking joints. When Nixon finally said the words "I shall resign..." champagne bottles were opened and other celebratory gestures took place around the park. A month later, when Nixon was pardoned for all possible crimes he may or may not have committed, the celebration was replaced by a weary reminder of how the nation was really run.

Chapter 4

Hell No We Won't Glow

In 1979, the Three Mile Island nuclear power plant near Harrisburg in western Pennsylvania headed towards meltdown. After a number of misleading newscasts de-emphasizing the nature and severity of the accident, it became clear that the warnings of the growing anti-nuclear movement were coming true. The energy industry really was willing to endanger all of us for their profits. A few weeks after the meltdown, one of the largest rallies against nuclear power to ever occur in the United States took place in Washington, DC. The speakers included Helen Caldicott and Jerry Brown. Artists who performed were Bonnie Raitt and John Sebastian. Later in the year, an even larger rally took place in New York City. In New England and California, grassroots organizations stepped up their campaigns against new plants then being constructed in Seabrook, New Hampshire and at Diablo Canyon in California. These grassroots groups (Clamshell Alliance at Seabrook, Abalone Alliance at Diablo Canyon) would develop into direct action campaigns that involved thousands of people blocking access to the plant construction sites in a multitude of ways. However, unlike their European counterparts, these protesters would ultimately insist on using only nonviolent methods and eventually merely script the direct actions with the authorities, creating protests that were nothing more than theater with an outcome already planned and the impact severely diminished.

Meanwhile in Germany, pitched battles took place between nuclear power opponents and police employed to defend the plants and their corporate ownership. The antinuclear movements were populated by an amalgam of farmers, environmentalists, anti-militarists, leftists and anarchists. The long hair of the Sixties counterculture and the punk styles of the 1970s were present in almost equal amounts at many of the actions. The rhetoric in the United States tended toward a post-Marxist/neo-hippie/liberal decentralism, while in Europe, it was a more Marxist and left-anarchist analysis that tended to dominate the conversation. These political differences would be part of what made the protests different, as well. It can also be argued that the difference in politics also made the European protests more effective in changing the popular mindset regarding nuclear power.

Generally speaking, the protests in Europe tended to be more overtly confrontational. This was especially the case in Germany, where the Autonomen not only moved the political analysis of the protests leftward, but also ramped up the level of confrontation. Autonomen were primarily young people determined not only to fight the power structure but to also live a life of revolutionary change. To this end they occupied (squatted) empty buildings and rehabilitated them, creating intentional communities in formerly desolate city blocks of several German cities. They set up cooperative groceries, bars, performance spaces, schools and childcare. The squats occasionally came under attack by police operating at the command of speculators and their political allies. At protests against nuclear power, the Autonomen and their allies came ready to fight. They were also crucial to the semi-permanent community of treehouses, lean-tos and other shelters established in opposition to government plans to expand the Frankfurt Airport. This community held the ground for more than two years and, besides providing a place for many hundreds of youths to live, also served as a staging ground for protests against the airport expansion and counterculture festivals. As the June 1981 police attack on airport squatters community proved (along with numerous raids in the 1970s on squatters' communities around Germany), the police were more than happy to meet the challenge presented by the Autonomen. In the United States, even the most confrontational protests were determinedly non-violent. Examining the Seabrook and Diablo Canyon actions makes this quite clear.

The first major protests in the Unites States against nuclear power took place in Seabrook, New Hampshire. After a legal rally organized by the Clamshell Alliance against the Seabrook plant in 1976, a small group of protesters returned and tried to occupy the construction site. The protesters adhered to strict rules of nonviolence and several were arrested during the action. A couple weeks after the original occupation attempt, even more protesters came back and attempted another occupation. A year later, at least 2500 protesters showed up for another occupation. The group had expanded not only its numbers but also its organization. The basic organization revolved around small groups of friends or otherwise connected individuals that formed themselves into affinity groups. These affinity groups would then choose a spokesperson or two to represent them in the spokescouncil, which was made up of representatives from each affinity group. All decisions would be reached at every level by consensus. At times an unwieldy process, the construction of the organization and the practice of consensus enabled smaller groups a fair amount of autonomy and creativity while simultaneously presenting a unified presence to the public and media. They set up a tent city that was called Freebrook by its inhabitants. It was at Freebrook where organized nonviolent actions on and near the plant site were planned.

As mentioned above, the insistence on passive nonviolence bordered on the pathological at times. This insistence stemmed in part from an understanding popular at the time (and pretty much ever since) among left-leaning protest groups that the New Left failed because it turned to violence. While this was certainly true to the extent that the glorification of violence by some New Left groups and individuals had turned off many people, this perspective tended to group any type of confrontation that included militant challenges to the authorities and the right wing as violent. Consequently, any action other than obeisance to the police was usually considered to transgress the nonviolence code required by the protest leadership.

In Europe it was different, especially in Germany. Decidedly more politically informed than its counterpart in the United States, the German countercultural left represented a large part of the radical wing of the anti-nuclear movement. The Greens, who tended toward pacifism, were the bulk of that part of the movement aligned with a political party. To their credit, the Greens maintained a policy of non-criticism of the militants' tactics. The militants consisted of the Rote Zelle (Revolutionary Cells), the Autonomen, and various communist groups. It was the Autonomen that tended to identify most strongly with the counterculture ethic of living outside the law. Already used to physically defending their squats in German cities and fighting with police at demonstrations around German abortion laws, laws restricting employment to leftists and protests against the persecution of the Red Armee Fraktion, the militants came ready to rumble. Besides the opposition to nuclear power, the movement was also seen by thousands of youth across class lines as a place to challenge the state. As the decade wore into the 1980s, divisions grew between the Greens and the militants, in large part because the Greens became more mainstream and moved away from their previously left-oriented politics. This dynamic also revealed itself in the squatters' communities and the "alternativ" neighborhoods adjacent to the squats. While the squatters maintained their anti-establishment politics and existence, the "Alternativ" neighbors kept their Birkenstocks, organic food and alternative living practices but rejected the confrontational stance of the Autonomen and their allies. Instead, the Alternativs tried to negotiate settlements with local authorities regarding housing and similar questions, hoping to eventually be able to purchase homes, thereby accepting the capitalist dynamic in place. Despite this growing divide, the level of militancy at anti-nuclear and other protests remained much higher in most European nations than at any time in the United States.

The philosophy known as ecofeminism was influential in the US protests. One of its main proponents, writer and pagan spiritualist Starhawk, was very involved with the organizational meetings leading up to the actions at Diablo Canyon in California. Her presence at the staging camp during the action was welcomed by most and was further testimony to the influence of this brand of feminist thought in the US antinuclear movement. Based on counterculture ethics that viewed the Earth as a living entity not to be roped off and raped, the metaphor of the earth mother represented this realm of thought well. Starhawk's Pagan spirituality rejected the Abrahamic religions' insistence on the father and replaced the omnipotent cruelty associated with that patriarchal sky-god with the ostensibly more nurturing goddess Gaia. Consequently, this form of paganism demanded a spirited defense of the planet.

Anarchists were also present in the US protests. In general, US anarchists tended to be less leftist than their European counterparts, leaning instead towards a more individualist lifestyle politics. Despite this general tendency, the primary anarchist organization present in both the Clamshell and Abalone alliances was the left-anarchist Love and Rage group. Unlike most US anarchists, Love and Rage most often worked as a unified group instead of as individuals. They recognized anarchism's leftist roots and organized along those lines. Because of its organized presence Love and Rage was often the deciding factor in blocking some of the more right-wing proposals floated at the Abalone Alliance's Diablo Canyon direct action in September 1981. I assume their practice was similar in New Hampshire. A small example of how this worked occurred in the Diablo Canyon group encampment. Some protesters were flying the US flag upside down near the entrance to the camp. Other groups were flying it right side up and asked those flying it upside down to turn their flags around so as not to alienate liberals. This latter group refused. The topic was brought up at an evening council meeting. If it had not been for the Love and Rage members present and a few independent individuals blocking the liberals demand, the proposal would have passed. Instead, a lively discussion ensued regarding the dynamics of protest, the meaning of the US flag and the nature of coalitions. The flag issue exposed the liberal nature of the Clamshell Alliance and the antinuclear movement in general. Unlike their counterparts in the German Green party, who expressed support for the militant wing of the movement in its early years, US liberals (many from the progressive wing of the Democratic Party) constantly tried to push radical elements out of the movement.

The Nuclear Industry and Mainstream Politics

As far as much of the mainstream political establishment was concerned, there was nothing wrong with nuclear power and, if there was, it could be easily fixed by a tweak here or there. Naturally, some of this opinion was the result of the money that flowed from the nuclear industry into the campaign coffers of elected officials. To this element of US society, the antinuclear movement was seen as mostly composed of a minority of leftover hippies and naïve, fearful country folk. This perception and the forces pushing it were lampooned in an issue of Gregory Irons' underground comic Slow Death, a series that addressed impending ecological issues in an apocalyptic manner. The nuclear industry did its best to further this perception of its opponents in its media blitzes and advertising, thereby hoping to associate opposition to nuclear energy with a lunatic fringe.

Chapter 5

It's Only Rock and Roll

While politics seemed to slowly drain out of rock music, the music itself was being subdivided into smaller and smaller niches. While there had always been divisions between different forms of the music: pop and rock; psychedelic rock and hard rock; Beatles and Rolling Stones; and so on, the music was now atomizing into ever more rigid genres. In part, this was due to the fact that the audience for the music was larger than it had ever been. However, it was also because different bands were playing very different kinds of rock music. The musical roots inspiring rock music may have been the same but the hard rock Led Zeppelin played sounded different than the music made by The Band; and the music of the Grateful Dead was considerably different from that of Grand Funk Railroad. Likewise, none of these bands were playing music that sounded like punk rock. Like the New Left and its disintegration into smaller grouplets, each espousing their analysis or championing a certain identity, the rock culture was evolving (or devolving) into numerous different groups of fans supporting their favorite bands and often denigrating others. This form of fandom reminded one of the emnity between sports rivals and made just about as much sense to those not involved in the fray. The universality of the counterculture was becoming less universal. Then again, maybe that universality never existed, except in the minds of those who believed in it.

The year 1975 saw the sonic arrival of redneck politics via an increasingly popular genre the rock media labeled Southern Rock. The band that represented this fan base the best was Lynyrd Skynyrd. Fans of this music shared much of their outlook with the growing legions of hard rock fans who liked Aerosmith or Ted Nugent's raucous melodies. Politically, the libertarian elements of this music's fan base were often overshadowed by an underlying racism. Nugent, who had debuted with the Detroit band The Amboy Dukes, then intentionally rejected the counterculture scene in Michigan represented best by John Sinclair and the band MC5, began writing hard rock songs in the mid-1970s that were remarkable primarily for their lack of either musical or lyrical creativity. Simultaneously, Nugent's brand of music

Daydream Sunset

allowed a certain elemental emotion to emerge that could easily lead to a brawl, especially when mixed with alcohol and the macho swagger that seemed to be part of much rock music. Some critics labeled this rock genre "crotch rock" mostly because of its over-the-top machismo and overtly sexist lyrics. As Nugent roared through the decade, his public statements became more reactionary and racist. His music was tremendously popular among younger adolescents and bikers. I recall a festival at the Ontario Motor Speedway in southern California in 1978 where Nugent was one of the headliners. When he began his set with his hit at the time, "Cat Scratch Fever," I was literally lifted off my feet and propelled forward several yards by the motion of the crowd. Thousands of teenage girls wearing black leather rushed the stage along with hundreds of older males clad in the chains and leather chaps commonly considered part of biker gear.

In 1976, the southern rock band Lynyrd Skynyrd toured stadiums across the United States. The opening band, called Wet Willie, was also from the south. Both groups featured wailing blues-based guitar leads and lyrics championing a simpler, rural life. The world they described was one essentially invented by their antecedents, the Macon, Georgia-based Allman Brothers, but without the hippie ethos the Allmans were closely identified with. Lynyrd Skynyrd had released the FM hit "Sweet Home Alabama" a year or two earlier. This song featured a catchy rock melody with lyrics that featured an admonition to Canadian Neil Young (who composed the anti-slavery song "Southern Man") and other northerners to mind their own business. Judging from the sales of tickets to their shows and the sales of the album made from the tour, Skynyrd's music appealed to a lot of people. It is impossible to determine how much of the fandom was based on the searing three-guitar attack of the band and how much was in response to the band's pro-Southern lyrics. The songs celebrated a world of simple, Agrarian living, like that described in North American settler mythology. In terms of gender roles, men were supposed to be in command, and women could not be trusted. While some of the content was standard fare for rock music (especially the tales of treacherous women), certain lyrics were unique in their celebration of a life found primarily in the hills of America's south.

Willie Nelson never celebrated southern racism. However, there were those among his fans that did.[xiii] Although Nelson had been a songwriter for more than decade, penning hits like Faron Young's "Hello Walls" and Patsy Cline's "Crazy," Willie only began singing his own songs for the public in the late 1960s. Like Leon Russell's foray into country music with the 1973 album *Hank Wilson's Back,* Nelson's growing popularity during the 1970s and his spearheading (along with Waylon Jennings) of the Outlaw country music movement represented another example of the counterculture's expansion into cultural realms previously denied, while also attesting to its decentralization. It can be argued that the decentralization of the counterculture weakened its central tenets of peace and love (if those, in fact, were its central tenets) while encouraging greater tolerance from the more conservative mainstream culture. Longhaired country singers like Willie Nelson might have been beat up by country music fans a few years prior to the 1975 release of the album that put his name on the counterculture's (and Billboard magazine's) Top 40, *Red Headed Stranger*. Even though country musicians had accepted the styles of the counterculture and been playing music with some rockers since the late 1960s (Bob Dylan, The Byrds, Earl Scruggs, Johnny Cash, and numerous session men, to name a few), most country music fans still considered the anti-hippie lyrics of Merle Haggard's "Okie From Muskogee" as gospel when it came to dealing with the counterculture and its adherents.

Willie Nelson's place in the counterculture was cemented after he moved from Nashville to Austin, Texas in 1972. The main hippie drag in Austin was Guadalupe Street. There, the University of Texas students brought weed, music, and other countercultural trappings. Janis Joplin sang in Austin before she moved to San Francisco. The Thirteenth Floor Elevators brought psychedelia to Texas. Willie Nelson grew his hair, smoked weed and knew how to write a song. His unusual, vibrato singing voice and a finger-picking guitar style usually played on nylon strings appealed to the hippies, bikers and rednecks who hung out at the Greater Armadillo World Headquarters, a cavernous building with lots of beer taps and dime bag dealers. Like most other counterculture strips and neighborhoods, Austin's Guadalupe Street had lost most of whatever innocence it held by 1970. Bikers controlled some elements of the drug trade, while organized crime pushed independent weed smugglers and dealers out of town. Pimps trolled for runaways to prostitute and heroin made its dark presence known. The violence that usually accompanies such changes was becoming routine in the neighborhood.

Willie Nelson's music was a hip marriage between the hippie ethos and the country & western culture. His band included members of his family and friends. Partially because of his work and constant touring, Austin attracted a new breed of hippie to its environs.

A more obvious and perhaps more ominous racism than Lynyrd Skynyrd's admonition to Neil Young would rear its ugly head in some mid-decade statements by popular rockers in Britain. Guitarist Eric Clapton made comments in support of the political campaign against Asian and other non-white immigrants by British racist Enoch Powell. Later, Clapton modified his statements.[xiv] That was not in time to stall the rapid growth of the punk-based Rock Against Racism (RAR) movement that swept through Britain in the late 1970s. RAR began in response to the previously mentioned comments from Eric Clapton. These comments, along with earlier statements by David Bowie that seemed to champion the fascist political philosophy and Britain's National Front, a racist and fascist political party then experiencing a surge in popularity at the polls, enraged various individuals in the rock press and the punk/New Wave scene.[xv] By 1977, many of the biggest bands in the British new wave and punk scene were on board, playing RAR gigs around the Isles and publishing a large circulation magazine called *Temporary Hoarding*.

After months of organizing made considerably easier in large part because of the support of these bands, the RAR movement's biggest gig took place on April 20, 1978. Thousands of youth from all over Britain gathered in London's Victoria Park to listen and dance to new wave and punk bands and antiracist organizers. Although the concert, headlined by the New Wave band The Tom Robinson Group and punk rock's The Clash, was organized by Rock Against Racism, some socialist groups and the Anti-Nazi League linked up with RAR to put on the April 30, 1978 festival. As noted above, several of Britain's most popular bands were part of the movement by this time. These bands included the Clash, Steel Pulse, Stiff Little Fingers, Sham 69, the Tom Robinson Band, and the Sex Pistols. RAR was a genuinely popular movement. In the following week's local elections the National Front failed to win any seats. In July, Rock Against Racism staged a carnival in Manchester featuring reggae artists Steel Pulse and the Buzzcocks. In September another London concert took place in Brixton's Brockwell Park with Stiff Little Fingers, Aswad and Elvis Costello. By the end of 1978, RAR had organized 300 local concerts and five carnivals, including the April 30th gig. In the run up to the 1979 elections in Britain, RAR organized and funded a 'Militant Entertainment Tour' that featured 40 bands playing 23 concerts and covering more than 2,000 miles on the road.

British punkers enjoyed another well-publicized foray into politics in 1977. This was the year of the Queen's Silver Jubilee. The celebration marked Queen Elizabeth's twenty-fifth year on the throne and, according to the Crown's press releases, was intended to unify the British nation and Commonwealth. The Silver Jubilee was also intended to convince a growing segment of the British population that the royal family was intrinsic to British identity and therefore worth the cost. In 1977, Britain was economically depressed and the Harold Wilson's Labor government was in its death throes, barely surviving a parliamentary no-confidence vote. Margaret Thatcher and the Tories were sharpening their knives, preparing for an all-out assault on public services. This assault would be unveiled a mere two years later when Thatcher became Prime Minister and started attacking unions, selling off public assets and slashing public welfare rolls. The economic policy that began as Thatcherism would become known world-wide as neoliberalism.

The Sex Pistols released the single "God Save the Queen" on May 27, 1977. Despite their later insistence that the song and its release date had nothing to do with the Queen's Silver Jubilee, most of Britain believed it did. BBC and the Independent Broadcasting Company refused to play the record. Nevertheless, it reached Number One in the New Musical Express charts and number two on the BBC charts. Its lyrics compared the monarchy to a fascist regime and otherwise took England's aristocrats to task. Perhaps more important than the lyrics about the Queen were the song's final verses that repeated the words "No future" over and over. Those two words would become a phrase repeated frequently in the decade to come by youth throughout the West when they attempted to describe the ravaged world they had been left. Despite the anti-monarchist feeling among much of Britain's youth, there really were no organized protests against the queen, other than a few local manifestations at parties sponsored by the monarchy and its supporters.

Chapter 6

Mr. Natural Takes a Trip

I don't pretend that my experiences during the time period are representative of the vast majority of my peers. However, the fact that so many of the people I have run into since the 1970s tell similar stories lends credibility to the notion that I wasn't alone. In this spirit, let me tell you a little tale of a trip up the New Jersey Turnpike in September 1977.

The Grateful Dead had not played all summer. This was unusual, but probably had something to do with band rehearsals and members' personal lives. Anyhow, they were making up for the lack of summer shows with a festival at the Formula One racetrack in Englishtown, New Jersey on Labor Day weekend. Tens of thousands of folks had already purchased tickets to the one-day festival that also featured the Marshall Tucker Band and the New Riders of the Purple Sage. My friends and I gathered together at my place in suburban Maryland the evening of Friday, September 2nd. We divvied up the weed and decided who would ride with whom. Our caravan headed north out onto I-95. As we approached the raceway, we ran into more and more folks heading to the same event. At one highway rest stop in southern New Jersey I purchased a few hits of Mr. Natural LSD and dispensed it among those in our caravan who wanted to start tripping. By the time we stopped at a diner a few miles from the venue in northern New Jersey early the next morning, my hallucinations reminded me of the Hunter S. Thompson interlude in *Fear and Loathing in Las Vegas* where his fellow bar patrons looked like lizards.

After devouring some eggs and toast, my friends and I parked the car and began the eight-mile trek towards the concert site. I sold a bunch of weed on the way. When I finally got into the show after buying a ticket for five bucks, the first thing I did was purchase enough acid for all of my friends to enjoy. Twelve hours later, the raceway was deserted, except for a few thousand people who had nowhere to go or no way to get to where they were going. A few of my friends and I were among this latter group. The next morning we ran into some Yippies from the Bleecker Street collective on Manhattan's Lower East Side who were making breakfast with food they had taken from the abandoned vendor stands around the edge of the field. The New Jersey Englishtown show was one of the last big rock concerts that was not over-policed. In other words, the potential for anarchistic chance (always a part of any good rock and roll adventure) had not been planned out of existence by the promoters and security.

Also, in 1977 the punk scene was starting to make a little noise beyond its London, San Francisco, Los Angeles and New York origins. Naturally, most of those dancing to the Grateful Dead were unaware of this fact, while those bouncing off the concrete in punk rock dives had nothing but disparaging remarks for their Deadhead compatriots. Neither of these countercultural elements had caught the attention of most of the US population, who seemed resigned to the malaise Jimmy Carter would soon refer to in a speech for which he would be much maligned, mostly because he was telling the truth. The Grateful Dead show in Englishtown could have been the Sixties counterculture's last big free-for-all. In fact, as far as the east coast of the United States was concerned, it might have been its wake.

After the Woodstock Festival in August 1969, and despite the much publicized mayhem at the Altamont, California festival in December of that year, rock festivals bloomed like mushrooms in the rain in the early 1970s. Some of the larger festivals in the United States included the Atlanta Pop Festival, the Texas Pop Festival, and the Seattle Pop Festival. Overseas, there were also multiple festivals, including two very famous ones in Britain at the Isle of Wight and another that continues to this day at Glastonbury. Germany and France saw their share of these large concerts, too. Although most festivals were capitalist ventures designed to make a few entrepreneurs rich quickly, many of them turned into the exact opposite when the sites were overwhelmed with people determined to get in for free. This occasionally created serious conflicts between security and festivalgoers. At other sites, the promoters opened the gates with little or no protest, having made enough profit from advance ticket sales. In addition to conflicts between security and crowds, the fact that a lot of people did not think they should have to pay for their music angered some performers. In a scene preserved on film from the 1970 Isle of Wight gathering, Joni Mitchell scolds the audience after a moment where a rather crazed individual was dragged from the stage during her set. It was Mitchell's belief that the audience did not respect the work of the performers. Some saw Mitchell's diatribe and similar statements by a few other wealthy rock artists as evidence of a growing class divide between the rock musicians and the culture from which they had sprung. Whether or not this was the case, it could certainly be argued that rock was rapidly becoming much more of a business where the standard capitalist model applied. In other words, some people made money and the rest handed it over. In response to the incidents at the Isle of Wight and the perception that a class divide was growing between rock listeners and rock musicians, a group of hippies began the Glastonbury Festival, making it free for all in attendance. This idea spread throughout England until police and other officials shut them down in the late 1970s.[xvi]

In spite of the conflicts about profits and the grouchiness of some big name performers, the experience of the rock festival attendee was quite often a liberating one. These festivals often became what would be known by the 1990s as temporary autonomous zones. The sheer presence of so many people intent on enjoying the music and each other's company suspended traditional societal restrictions enforced by police, family and church. Instead, these large gathering fostered a feeling of belonging to a new type of community that kept chaos from breaking out. Perhaps there is no more perfect example of this self-imposed control than that found at a 1970 festival in Powder Ridge, Connecticut. Local authorities cancelled the festival at the last moment. At least thirty thousand people showed up anyhow. There was no electric music, no toilet facilities and no food for sale. However, most who attended enjoyed themselves and saw the festival as a gathering of their tribe. Police wisely chose not to try and clear the grounds, waiting until people left of their own accord. Naturally, various local and media people saw drug use and called for arrests, but were ignored. Dozens more festivals would be thwarted by authorities in the months to come, especially in the United States. Bill Mankin noted in a reminiscence he wrote for the website *Like the Dew* that "There was almost nowhere else than at a rock festival where it felt like one could tap so deeply and directly into the communal coronary artery of the counterculture. It was truly heady stuff."[xvii] That sentence does a lot to explain why the authorities wanted to close down rock festivals in the 1970s.

By the mid-1970s, rock festivals were almost non-existent, other than the occasional one-day concert at a motor speedway (like the Englishtown show introducing this chapter.) This type of festival was administered more like a stadium rock concert or even a football game than what people once expected from a rock festival. Planning and execution incorporated local law enforcement and civil authorities in their planning considerably more than before. In fact, local police in uniform often served as the security for these shows both inside and outside the venues. The presence of police inside shows naturally led to many more arrests and occasional confrontations. In the place of rock events, festival goers still hoping to find the earlier vibe of community and freakdom once experienced in rock concerts turned to bluegrass and folk festivals instead. Some of these folk and bluegrass concerts included electric rock bands. One example of such a festival was the Stompin' '76 event that took place near Galax, Virginia. This festival attracted a couple hundred thousand people and featured acts like Bonnie Raitt and David Bromberg. It took place despite the vocal opposition of some local citizens and the police. A little more than a year later, at least three similar events took place in Pennsylvania and Virginia without any problems from authorities or locals. Meanwhile, a festival featuring several rock bands in western Maryland was cancelled at the last minute by the local authorities, leaving a few thousand ticket buyers without music or a legal place to camp. Despite rumors that the police were going to force everyone from the site, the sheriff and his men were held back from doing so when law enforcement officials from neighboring communities refused to provide men for the raid.

Another, more intentionally counterculture event began in 1972, and was initially organized by commune dwellers and others involved in the counterculture wanting to create a temporary intentional primitive community in the wilderness. The first of these events—eventually called Rainbow Gatherings—took place in the Colorado Rockies and drew about two thousand people. Even though this gathering was supposed to be a one-time event, there was enough grassroots interest among the attendees and those who heard about the event to stage another the following year. Over the course of the decade, the Rainbow Gathering's attendance swelled in size to approximately 20,000. The event located itself in different national forests in late June and early July, with peak attendance usually during the first four days of July. Because of its decidedly counterculture character, it was usually opposed by some locals and law enforcement in whatever region it occurred. Also, like most counterculture happenings, there were a certain number of people wanted by police in attendance. The original event resulted in the birth of the Rainbow Family of Living Light, a loose-knit family of counterculture individuals scattered around the planet that probably numbers in the tens of thousands.

Essentially a spiritual conclave, the Rainbow Gathering sites contained no running water, toilets, or electricity. Their ethic was based on trust and a live and let live philosophy. Alcohol was forbidden in the main camp, but over the years those who wished to drink formed their own campsite on the fringes of the gathering territory. All decisions were supposed to be reached by the process of consensus and no official leaders existed, elected or otherwise. Rarely political, Rainbow Family members have organized themselves in opposition to marijuana laws and environmental destruction.

On September 8, 1979 hundreds of folks descended on the Monterey Fairgrounds in California for the Second Tribal Stomp Festival, organized by Chet Helms of San Francisco's Family Dog concert promotion collective. The Family Dog put on rock shows before Bill Graham entered the business and helped turn rock into the mega-business it is today. Helms and his cohort believed in the hippie ethos and considered profit as a necessary evil, at best. Graham, on the other hand, seemed to see profiteering as essential to his existence.

The first Tribal Stomp was held the year before at the University of California Berkeley's Greek Theatre. The show featured bands, poets and others associated with the counterculture of the 1960s. Country Joe and the Fish, Allen Ginsberg, Big Brother and the Holding Company and Gregory Corso were just a few of the acts on the stage that day. The second Tribal Stomp represented a different approach altogether. Organizers Helms and Graham hoped to bring together bands from the 1960s scene and intersperse their performances with sets by up-and-coming punk, new wave and alt-country bands. The promoters' desire was to create a common ground between the freak/hippie community and the punk rockers. In part, this desire stemmed from Helms' belief (and the belief of many others) that the punk ethos was quite similar to the Sixties counterculture in its opposition to the politics and culture of the Establishment. Another reason was an attempt to bridge a gap that the press was stirring up between the two groups. Unfortunately, the street was responding to these incitements, with punks harassing longhairs in locales they shared, and vice versa.

The bands Helms and Graham had lined up included The Clash,

Joe Ely, Soul Syndicate, Chambers Brothers, Nick Gravenites, Maria Muldaur, Peter Tosh, Lee Michaels, Big Mama Thornton, The Blues Project, Dan Hicks and His Hot Licks, and Country Joe and the Fish. The weather was beautiful. The cops were mostly low key, except when it came time to enforce the curfew. A Monterey cop pulled the plug on Peter Tosh and his band yet did nothing about the giant spliff in his mouth. However, hardly anyone showed up to the festival. When The Clash played, the audience inside the venue was primarily made up of punks, who did not stick around for most of the other bands. I listened to the Clash's set, being politically and intellectually curious and not opposed to punk music. However, the stares I received from the Mohawk-coiffed guys near me when I lit up one of the ready rolled joints I had almost caused me to extinguish it. But, I didn't. Back then, the concert space was always liberated turf when it came to reefer, even if the people next to the smoker didn't like it. Given their equal distaste for the police, at least I knew the punks weren't going to turn me in to the cops wandering outside the stage area. From all appearances, it seemed the idea of a gathering of the freak and punk elements of the counterculture was premature. It appeared that opposing styles took precedence over the commonalities between the two oppositional cultures. Instead of coalescing in opposition to the culture of suburbia, greed, and wars of conquest, the differences of opinion over hair and music controlled the dynamic. By the mid-1980s, this division would be minimized, especially in large urban areas with a vibrant punk scene.

Chapter 7

Where All the Pigs Have Tails

In 1969, Quicksilver Messenger Service, a rock group closely identified with the Haight Ashbury psychedelic scene (along with the Grateful Dead and Jefferson Airplane) recorded a song titled "Shady Grove." Musically akin to the bluegrass song of the same name, it succinctly describes why hippies were moving to the hills (to borrow a line from the Temptations song "Ball of Confusion"). In fact, the lyric that says it the best is when John Cippolina sings about getting away from the smog and traffic and enjoying the farm where "all the pigs have tails." The line was obviously a reference to the police. Unlike their less political brothers in the Grateful Dead, Quicksilver was not a stranger to political statements. Their song "What About Me?" was an anthem of politically-oriented freaks in the counterculture. Considerably less strident than the political material that appeared on Jefferson Airplane's 1969 *Volunteers* album, "What About Me?" is a plaintive call challenging the authorities to respond to the changes the countercultural revolutionaries were trying to make happen.

While urban countercultural neighborhoods were either dying or transitioning to a gentrified version of their recent past, communes and other types of collectives were being established in rural areas nearby. Northern California, Vermont, and some isolated regions in the US South became the sites of collective countercultural living experiments. Some were spiritual in nature, while others tended toward plain survival. Still others became gathering spots for urban nomads who desired a break from the city streets. In Vermont, a network of politically-inclined communes formed in the wake of a migration out of New York and Boston. Perhaps the best published chronicle of this migration and attempts to establish a communal life in Vermont is the book *Total Loss Farm* by Liberation News co-founder Raymond Mungo.

Even in the woods, there was political organizing going on. The prime example of this is the Free Vermont movement initiated by members of the Red Clover Commune of Putney, Vermont. Begun by media activists and members of the New Left media collective Newsreel, including Jane Kramer, Roz Payne, John Douglas and

Robert Kramer, this commune moved to Vermont near the beginning of what became known as the back-to-the-land movement. It was one of a few dozen communes that would sprout around the state of Vermont. Like their philosophical neighbors out west, the members were urban refugees (many of whom were suburban refugees first) and had little understanding of the daily and seasonal struggles of living in the country. According to a former Vermont communard Robert Houriet, "The first phase was an escape, but it was an escape which had a utopian element... The big bang came after the Chicago [Democratic National] Convention. The Chicago convention [and the ensuing riots] was the epigamic event where people realized the political movement was over –fractured beyond repair. You can go to the Weathermen or you can go to Vermont."[xviii]

The earlier communards had moved out of the city to get away from the hassles of the street and, in many cases, the police and political repression against their lifestyle and politics. After 1968, the early trickle of migrants became a flood. They left behind established networks of friends and political allies, leaving many feeling isolated and alienated in their new environs. This was especially true in Vermont when winter came, literally stranding people without roads, heat or a means to get around. Red Clover Commune was among the first of the Vermont communes to realize that the only way to prevent this alienation was to organize the communards around the state. So they began the Free Vermont movement, organizing food buying coops across the state, arming themselves for the revolution they believed was coming and establishing a popular statewide Left/counterculture newspaper with a print run of several thousand.

Other Free Vermont institutions included a free auto shop (Liberation Garage) a worker-owned and operated restaurant (the Common Ground), a free health clinic in Burlington, a school called Red Paint in southern Vermont and a Peoples' Bank. They organized forums against the war. Members also organized women's groups and groups dedicated to ecological issues. According to George van Deusen's historical article from the Catamount Tavern News Service, "The success of these endeavors varied, but for a few years, perhaps between 1969-1973, one could squint their eyes and almost see the outline of a true cultural revolution on the horizon. Free Vermont, though counting a hardcore activist base of no more 100, soon attracted ten times that many fellow travelers; a sizable force in a state that at that time had a total population of less than 400,000 people."[xix]

No other region of the country experienced a comparable politically-oriented commune movement. However, this did not mean that there were no other communes. Some, like the Farm in Summertown, Tennessee, were spiritual in their inspiration, while others were motivated by a desire to live off the land with extended families. After establishing itself in Tennessee, the Farm went on to provide midwifing services and a place for pregnant young women who did not want abortions (or could not get them due to the law) to have their child and to leave it if they chose. Tolstoy Farm in eastern Washington established a working organic farm. It was also a place where individuals could purchase a piece of land by participating in the collective endeavors of the commune. After an agreed upon number of years of working residency, members could then build a home as long as they remain involved in the farm's common pursuits. The Hog Farm, meanwhile, formed out of the Merry Pranksters after Ken Kesey exiled himself to Mexico to avoid arrest. After the Woodstock festival, where the Hog Farm served as a "security" force, the group purchased and outfitted some buses and began traveling and working rock festivals around the nation. By the mid-1970s, they were residing more or less permanently in Berkeley, California and Taos, New Mexico, where they engaged in political and countercultural activities and worked with another longstanding communal group, the Grateful Dead. In addition, they began operating a phone answering service in Berkeley known as the Babylon Answering Service to pay their mortgage.

In a confluence of the feminist and the back to the land movements, a group of women communards in California began a newspaper called *Country Women*. Part of the community of communes in northern California that became known as New Albion, this collective was but one of several that came and went during the late 1960s and 1970s along the Albion coast of Mendocino County. Though less political than their Free Vermont counterparts, the communes in this part of California attempted to organize themselves along similar lines. Food buying networks, resource sharing and other forms of co-operativism helped these communes grow and survive the decade. Of course, winters in California are considerably more temperate than those in Vermont and the rest of the Northeast. This meant that survival proved less challenging. On the downside, this also meant that some of these communes had to put up with an excess of drifters, many of whom contributed little or nothing to the general well-being. While the ethos of the counterculture expressed tolerance for those who did not contribute, the practicality of having folks hanging around using limited resources often pushed the levels of forbearance.

People's Park in Berkley represented a multitude of concepts to a multitude of people. To hippies, it represented a garden in the city and a place to hang out that had been created by the people. To politicos, it was a piece of liberated land, taken back from the power elites in a true uprising and held via a people's effort that represented the best and the worst of the revolution. To the University of California authorities and Ronald Reagan, People's Park represented all that was wrong with the counterculture and its allies. As far as the elites were concerned, there was no respect for private property or the police hired to protect it. What right, thought this group and those that supported them, do they have to take over land that was owned by the university and turn it into a park? The counterculture's answer was the now famous broadsheet composed and distributed by members of the ad hoc group that inspired the park in the first place. The text of the leaflet began, "Someday a petty official will appear with a piece of paper, called a land title, which states that the University of California owns the land of the People's Park. Where did that piece of paper come from? What is it worth?" The leaflet ended with a challenge: "We are building a park on the land. We will take care of it and guard it, in the spirit of the Costanoan Indians. When the University comes with its land title we will tell them: 'Your land title is covered with blood. We won't touch it. Your people ripped off the land from the Indians a long time ago. If you want it back now, you will have to fight for it again.'" The park would become the site of several more battles over the next decade, primarily because the university thought it could take it back from the residents who had actually turned it into a public space. The final battle of the decade occurred in the autumn of 1979.

The showdown was, like most of those previous, provoked by the university. Despite agreements between the city of Berkeley, a park committee composed of students, park denizens, local residents who as served caretakers, and the community in general, the administration decided to turn the free parking lot in the park's west end into a pay lot. The afternoon before the meters were to be put in place, a couple dozen members of the University of California police force escorted a bulldozer into the park and began removing benches. The bulldozer was phase one. One of the park's denizens – a big mean guy named Tommy Trashcan — walked over to the dozer and pulled out the ignition wires. I never liked the fellow before or after that act, but at that moment he was my hero. The police attempted to arrest him as more cruisers arrived. After a twenty-minute tussle, Trashcan was hauled into the police van. The cop vehicle was immediately surrounded by a couple dozen folks, who sat on the ground around the van. The cop at the wheel revved his engine and charged through the crowd. After that, somebody went to the tool shed in the bushes at the other end of the lot and brought out a couple of pickaxes. The people there took turns removing the asphalt in the parking lot piece by piece. After a series of unheeded warnings to those digging, the cops left, bragging that they would win and take the park back.

Before dawn the next morning several hundred enraged citizens hung around in the park and the surrounding sidewalks. Despite the previous afternoon's activity, the University had installed machines overnight that dispensed tickets at the entrances to the parking lot overnight. Some protesters passed out leaflets urging drivers to park elsewhere, some drank an early morning beer, and some sharpened sticks for use in the attack they felt sure was coming. In the parking lot across Haste Street were the police. Perhaps a hundred cops milled around drinking coffee, putting on their riot gear and talking on their radios. They were preparing for battle as seriously as those looking for one on the other side of the street. The adrenalin levels were high all around.

About half an hour before the University had commanded the new pay parking lot to open, a bus from the Hog Farm, known as the Asp, arrived on the scene. While some of the park's swarthier defenders removed the machines demanding parking fees from the earth, the Asp's inhabitants began handing out balloons and tying a string of them around the park. Those in the park smiled a little, the tension eased a bit by the Hog Farmers' antics. As far as the throng of police officers across the street were concerned, however, their intent didn't seem to change. Indeed, their desire to attack only seemed to be enhanced by the Hog Farmers' lightheartedness.

As the defining moment approached, Salty, a member of the park's organizing and maintenance committee, spoke on the phone to the mayor, Communist Party member Gus Newport. The Hog Farmers continued to distribute balloons. Somebody, maybe it was

Wavy Gravy, was playing reveille on a kazoo. While the Hog Farmers were finding plenty of takers among the citizens in the park and those who came to park, they couldn't even pay one of the cops to take even one balloon. Just as the riot squad moved into their attack formation and pulled down the clear plastic visors on their helmets, the mayor drove up. He got out of his car and waved good morning to the park's defenders. Then he told the police to leave. Since he was the city cops' boss they did so, cursing, one can be sure, the commie son of a bitch all the way back to their cars. This left behind a much-reduced force of University police who could do little but observe. This they did for six weeks.

During those six weeks the parking lot was removed piece by piece and the beginnings of a garden were put in place. The occupation of the park enjoyed tremendous support for the first month. The first couple weeks' worth of evenings, in fact, turned into big picnics with folks from all around the Bay Area bringing food, beer, pot and music makers. Merriment reigned those nights as people met new friends and hung out with old ones. Professionals with loosened ties on their way home from work joined together with hardened park habitués, musicians, college students and brothers from the streets of Oakland and West Berkeley. Everyone began to plant a garden where the parking lot had been. Local businesses brought donations of plants and building supplies. As time went on, though, the picnics got smaller, and eventually the only people who remained were those who had nowhere else to go. This was mostly a collection of street people, petty criminals who made their living from selling real or bogus dope to tourists, and hard-core gypsies. Two days after Thanksgiving the cops moved in and sent everyone on their way. Some went back to jail and some went to the hospital. Others headed to the freeway entrance at the end of Berkley's University Avenue to join the rest of the hitchhikers seeking a ride out of town. In the wake of the occupation, the anger remained. So did the garden planted in that former parking lot. The park continued to be the site of rock concerts and other community gatherings, some of which also provoked pitched battles between police and community members, usually after police had interfered with an event.

Religion and the Counterculture

Although this book has refrained from discussing the move many hippies made from the counterculture into various strains of organized religion, besides journeys like Chicago 7 defendant Rennie Davis's conversion to the Guru Maharaji sect, it is worth mentioning one other instance, if only because of its tragic end. Peoples Temple was located in San Francisco and recruited among the Bay Area's poor, lost and alternative thousands. The leader, Jim Jones, preached a communitarian philosophy that was non-judgemental and seemed open to all. Most of the members lived communally and shared everything. Jones encouraged leftist political activism and openly supported candidates and campaigns championing social justice. His followers did the same. However, as time went on, Jones's actions became more paranoid and bizarre. Temple members began to leave, telling stories of sexual abuse and violent reprimands for opposing Jones' increasingly bizarre edicts. Politicians began to question Jones' project and the Temple made plans to move to South America. In October 1978, San Francisco and the world were shocked to learn of a mass suicide/homicide taking place at the Temple's commune in Guyana. Over 800 people died, including several hundred children.

Chapter 8

Food for People

The Food Conspiracy network in the San Francisco Bay Area was a template for how a food co-op could be built. What began as a couple of bulk food buying clubs set up by collectives of people living together turned into an entire network of bulk food buying clubs organized in opposition to the corporate world of supermarkets and pesticide laced goods. The biggest of these networks in the Bay Area was the one organized and maintained by the White Panther commune on Page Street in the Haight district of San Francisco. The first place I lived in the Bay Area was in East Oakland, not far from the park the city called DeFremery Park and the people called Bobby Hutton Park after the murdered Black Panther. One of my housemates was a communist and Food Conspiracy worker. Every week he would head up to the Earth People's Park Commune in West Berkeley to meet the food delivery truck from San Francisco. When the truck arrived, my housemate, a few Earth Peoples Park members and some White Panthers would break the food down into separate orders and then wait until each household had collected their food. This network lasted for more than a decade distributing food to hundreds, if not thousands of people throughout the Bay Area, despite persistent police harassment of the White Panther commune by San Francisco police. Although the Food Conspiracy network did not evolve into any stores, this was an anomaly. In most places that had developed a network of buying clubs, an actual storefront usually resulted.

Another instance of food and politics mobilizing a community occurred at the University of Maryland College Park during the 1974-1975 academic year. By 1970, this somewhat suburban university town had been recognized as a New Left recruiting ground and, for longhairs in the DC area, as a countercultural haven. Along with Takoma Park and the Georgetown district of Washington, DC, College Park was a safe place for hippies and their culture. There were a couple friendly bars, a head shop called Maggie's Farm, bookstores that sold the latest underground papers, a health food store, and always a fair amount of weed and other drugs. The campus had a large radical contingent and counterculture values were well-represented in the student body. However, the university administration was quite reactionary. Campus and county police raided the dorms every spring, busting dozens of students for drugs. These raids usually caused students and local Yippies to riot in protest. During the early 1970s, the stretch of US Route 1 near the university was shut down every spring in protest of the war. Campus and state officials called the National Guard into town and campus each spring from 1970-1972.

In the fall of 1974, radicals ran the student government in College Park, Maryland. The president, Marc Strumpf, was allegedly a member of Youth Against War and Fascism and known to enjoy countercultural pursuits. The vice president of the student body was another countercultural radical. The food service was completely controlled by the Macke Corporation and the food was reminiscent of the stuff served in prisons and army mess halls, starchy, mushy and greasy. Some of the hippie students started making healthy sandwiches and muffins and selling them in front of the Student Union building. The student government and the two nearby food coops, Glut Food Coop and Rainbow Food Coop, supported them. The university administration told the campus cops to shut down the sandwich selling because it violated the exclusive food service contract held by Macke Corporation. After the cops seized the sandwiches and ordered the sandwich sellers to cease and desist, most of the Left organizations on campus joined in the protest against the harassment. The students continued to sell sandwiches and the administration continued to arrest the sandwich sellers. The protests continued as well, growing in size as students grew angry over the administration's intransigence and refusal to reconsider the food service contract. Eventually, the sandwich sellers won and a food coop was built in the Student Union basement using student-paid fees. A record coop was also established, providing albums and accessories at a discount price since the coop was an anti-profit store. Meanwhile, the Rainbow Food Coop closed down in part because of a shift in the grocery buying demographics in its locality.

New food coops continued to open across the United States, especially in university towns and rural areas experiencing a migration of counterculture types. Despite corporate opposition from supermarket chains, the coops survived, in large part because of the allegiance of their customer/owners. Another aspect of the food coop and the back-to-the-land movements was a renewed interest in healthier food and food production. This element did not require a rejection of the profit motive like coop membership and was therefore much more incorporated into mainstream society as time passed. Small companies making alternative food products grew quickly between 1970 and the 1980s, with several eventually being swallowed up by much larger corporations once their profits became too great for those corporations to ignore.

The White Panther Party

Like the Yippies, the White Panthers began as counterculture radicals determined to politicize the hippies and freaks constantly being harassed, locked up and beaten by cops just for the way they looked and acted. Arising from the bohemian scenes in Detroit and Ann Arbor, Michigan, and led by John and Leni Sinclair, the White Panthers wrote a manifesto, helped put together a rock band, and organized music festivals, protest rallies and food co-ops in the two cities. The police reacted rather viciously in Detroit, busting members' houses and concerts put on by the group. The Detroit cadre moved to Ann Arbor. John Sinclair was arrested for giving two joints to a narc in 1969. He was sentenced to ten years in prison. His case became a cause celebre in the counterculture, attracting the support of Abbie Hoffman, John and Yoko Ono Lennon, and a quality legal team. Some members moved to San Francisco, where they squatted a house in the Haight Ashbury district, organized a food buying network called the Food Conspiracy, free meals in the Golden Gate Panhandle, free concerts in the Haight and on Telegraph Avenue in Berkeley, and helped locals organize tenants' unions and rent strikes. The San Francisco group was nominally led by a man named Tom Stevens. As the Haight turned uglier and street crime increased, Stevens and the Panthers organized self-defense classes and patrols. The city police took exception to the patrols and harassed members of the group, especially Stevens. Residents, however, supported the Panther house and helped defend it against attempts to evict the Panthers. Like the Black Panthers, the White Panthers, especially the San Francisco group, believed in the right to armed self-defense. This position led them to oppose gun control laws enacted by the liberal/progressive City Council and even into a couple confrontations with the police. Stevens and another Panther Terry Phillips, spent three years in San Quentin after a shoot-out in 1974. In a time when much of the counterculture was non-political, the White Panthers and the Yippies seemed to become more determined than ever in keeping the political pressure on.

Chapter 9

Womyn Break the Bonds

The counterculture was liberatory, for some more than others. Foremost among those who got shortchanged in the dawning of the Aquarian age were women and girls. Nothing makes this clearer than the songs of the culture. From the macho posturing of songs like "Hey Joe" to the hippie mama mellowness of the Grateful Dead's "Sugar Magnolia," it was clear that the counterculture was, as the song says, a man's world. Although the sexual liberation prevalent in the communes, collectives and elsewhere created space for women to explore and express themselves sexually in ways not previously acceptable, it also did little to discourage predatory males from exploiting and taking advantage of them. Simultaneously, the assumption that women were somehow less capable than men remained prevalent. Of course the primary shareholders in this were men, but like their sisters in the dominant culture many counterculture women accepted, or at least tolerated, the imbalance. However, the growing feminist wave was beginning to create some gender schisms among the freaks, in both personal and public settings. Of course, this caused friction between the genders, just as it did in the New Left.

Perhaps the most public attack on men's sexist attitudes in the New Left/counterculture appeared in the All Women's Issue of the New York underground paper *The RAT*. This issue appeared in March, 1970 and included some brutally written attacks on the macho revolutionary stereotype many new leftists were adopting, the use of movement women as secretaries and cooks, and the general refusal of the "male-dominated Left" to take women and their contributions seriously. In addition, it attacked the hippie goddess and earth mother archetypes present in the counterculture. The cover essay, written by Robin Morgan, remains a classic piece of feminist separatist rhetoric.

Although Morgan's polemic was mostly concerned with the Left, she also saved a couple of slashing paragraphs for the counterculture, unleashing a torrent of words directed at men and some of the attitudes found in basic hippie ideology. I reproduce some excerpts here:

"Goodbye to Hip culture and the so-called Sexual Revolution, which has functioned toward women's freedom as did the Reconstruction toward former slaves—reinstituting oppression by another name. ...Goodbye to the assumption that Hugh Romney is safe in his cultural revolution, safe enough to refer to our women, who make all our clothes without somebody not forgiving that.... Goodbye to Tuli and the Fugs and all the boys in the front room— who always knew they hated the women they loved. Goodbye to the notion that good ol' Abbie is any different from any other up- and-coming movie star who ditches the first wife and kids, good enough for the old days but awkward once you're Making It. Good- bye to his hypocritical double standard that reeks through the tattered charm. Goodbye to lovely "pro-Women's Liberationist" Paul Krassner, with all his astonished anger that women have lost their sense of humor "on this issue" .... Run it down. Goodbye to a beautiful new ecology movement that could fight to save us all if it would stop tripping off women as earthmother types or frontier chicks, if it would right now cede leadership to those who have not polluted the planet because that action implies power and wom- en haven't had any power in about 5,000 years, cede leadership to those whose brains are as tough and clear as any man's but whose bodies are also unavoidably aware of the locked-in rela- tionship between humans and their biosphere—the earth, the tides, the atmosphere, the moon. Ecology is no big shtick if you're a woman—it's always been there.

"Goodbye to the complicity inherent in the Berkeley Tribesmen being part publishers of Trashman Comics; goodbye, for that mat- ter, to the reasoning that finds whoremaster Trashman a fitting model, however comic-strip far-out, for a revolutionary man.... Goodbye to the New Nation and Earth Peoples Park for that mat- ter, conceived by men, announced by men, led by men—doomed before birth by the rotting seeds of male supremacy transplanted into fresh soil. Was it my brother who listed human beings among the objects that would be easily available after the Revolution: Free grass, free food, free women, free acid, free clothes, etc.? Was it my brother who wrote Fuck your women till they can't stand up and said that groupies were liberated chicks 'cause they dug a

tit-shake instead of a handshake? The epitome of male exclusion-ism—men will make the Revolution—and make their chicks. Not my brother. No. Not my revolution. Not one breath of my support for the new counterfeit Christ—John Sinclair. Just one less to worry about for ten years. I do not choose my enemy for my brother..." [xx]

As this excerpt makes apparent, the counterculture and its political counterpart needed some feminist enlightenment. While some of Morgan's criticism seems contradictory (her swipe at Hoffman stands out in this regard given the obvious patriarchal nature of marriage itself), the essence of it was just begging to be said. For those with enough of a conscience to care about this issue, much of the 1970s would be spent working on changing the obviously sexist dynamic Morgan railed against. Others in the counterculture, would spend their time either rationalizing their sexism or ignoring it.

It's worth examining the sexism engrained in the values of the counterculture, especially in relation to its oppositional nature. If nothing else, the fact that so many of the assumptions held by the dominant culture regarding women were replicated in the counterculture proves how subconscious and universal such attitudes really were. At the same time, the liberation felt by women who participated in the counterculture may in some way have propelled many of them to reconsider their roles. This was true on both an individual and societal level. When women began to control their sexual lives, they found themselves expecting more autonomy in their public lives too, in the counterculture and beyond. However, like their sisters in the New Left, women in the counterculture found their expectations challenged from within and without their social sphere. In other words, many of their so-called brothers were not ready to give up their male privilege. Indeed, like their brethren in the New Left, many counterculture males were unwilling to confront their own sexism.

Of course, the prevalence of sexist attitudes in the music, literature and film popular in the counterculture did nothing to counter individual male's own attitudes. From the occasionally dismissive lyrics of the Rolling Stones, Bob Dylan and other major rock acts to the growing numbers of those artists whose lyrics portrayed women as earth mothers, naive waifs, and just plain old hippie chicks, there were very few perspectives that did not attempt to pigeonhole the roles of women and girls in counterculture society. In addition, there was the reportage in the rock press of rock star cocksmanship and mistreatment of female fans. There were plenty of reasons to be angry for women fed up with the counterculture, just as there were few examples inside the culture for men wishing to perceive women as equals and agents of their own lives.

Morgan's diatribe in *The RAT*, repeated in discussions within communities and between individuals wherever freaks and hippies gathered, did shake things up. Over time other underground papers picked up the call, calling on rock fans to "stop supporting the blatant sexists of rock... They only perpetuate what is vile and unhealthy in our culture."[xxi] Relationships splintered and new ones formed. Many women found themselves questioning their previous preferences and explored same-sex relationships. Expected roles inside communes and other collective living arrangements were also challenged, whether those roles had to do with childrearing, housework or making money. In some communes the challenge from women was met with resistance, while other communal communities adapted over time, preferring to keep the greater family together. One commune that seemed to have adjusted was the Hog Farm, nominally led by Hugh Romney (neé Wavy Gravy,) one of the targets of Morgan's attack piece. However, many others collapsed under the weight of the conflicts created by women asserting change. In his article about the Vermont communes gathered under the Free Vermont banner, David van Dusen discussed the influence of the new feminist movement in those communes.

> "Internally, a good number if not most communes sought to break the subtle and not so subtle chains of sexism. More often than not (and as a rule on Free Vermont Communes), decisions were made democratically, by all the members, housework was expected from males, while tasks such a splitting winter wood was also done by women. Childcare was collectivized and was performed by both sexes. Political meetings would include woman's caucuses. ...However, their efforts did not result in perfection. Female communard, Lou Andrews, recalls her days on the rural Franklin Commune (which was a core Free Vermont commune) as a time where she felt more liberated than previously in mainstream society, but one where men still had a disproportionate influence upon the general direction of the commune. In her opinion this

*influence was a subconscious force; one that was not guaranteed
by formal process, but one that existed none the less."[xxii]*

Such a force would be harder to combat than something more formalized and helps explain why women felt the need to separate themselves not only from a communal situation but also from men in general since this subconscious force was prevalent throughout society.

According to Gretchen Lemke-Santangelo in her study *Daughters of Aquarius: Women of the Sixties Counterculture*, counterculture women were more likely to adopt a feminism "that affirmed and celebrated 'natural' or 'essential' female characteristics, in contrast to the radical feminist position that gender, as a social construct, was at the roots of women's oppression."[xxiii] In practice, this meant that counterculture women saw their roles as equal but quite different. Allegedly female attributes like tolerance, nurturing and harvesting were celebrated and presented to the culture as equivalent to physical strength, business acumen and whatever other attributes might be considered male. In addition, they insisted that attributes once considered as being those of the male could also be shared by females, and vice versa. This was a liberating claim.

One phenomenon that came more or less directly from the feminist and gay liberation movements was that of identity politics. While it is somewhat possible to trace the origins of these politics back to the Black Liberation movement, the fact of that movement's roots in anti-racism provides a counter to that argument. Identity politics true genesis seems to have derived historically from the two subsequent movements. This is not to say that there were not powerful components of the women's and gay liberation movements whose political interpretation of these groups' oppression leaned more towards a Left analysis. However, by the late 1970s, the dominant approach in the feminist movement was what the Left called bourgeois feminism. Best represented by the magazine *Ms.*, this approach emphasized the pursuit of women's individual and professional goals while ignoring the more basic issues of gender equality faced by working and poor women. The left wing of the feminist movement continued to agitate around the latter issues, which included childcare, equal pay, free birth control and abortion, and other issues relating to survival. These leftists were occasionally joined by their separatist sisters in the movement. Indeed, sometimes the two categories were indistinct.

The bourgeois feminist movement was seen as a white and middle-class movement that addressed the situation of women who were well educated, financially solvent, and ambitious. Their struggles centered on breaking the glass ceiling in management and public affairs. Their antecedent was the woman described in Betty Friedan's classic text *The Feminine Mystique*. The elements of feminism they shared with their separatist and working class sisters (often women of color) were the daily harassment and belittling of their personhood, the legal and de facto prejudices against their gender, and the negative portrayal of their gender in the media. The elements they did not share were associated with class and race. This division would widen as the decade progressed and the plight of working class women became more economically difficult.

One of the key feminist struggles of the decade was the movement to get the Equal Rights Amendment added to the US Constitution. The essential part of this amendment read "Equality of rights under the law shall not be denied or abridged by the United States or by any state on account of sex." It was supported by almost every Democrat and opposed by a number of Republicans. The primary popular opposition was a well-funded effort spearheaded by right-wing activist Phyllis Schlafly. However, there were some women labor leaders and other traditionally left-leaning groups that also opposed it. Their opposition was primarily based on traditional perceptions of women's roles at the time, and the complementary belief that women needed special protections to preserve the roles of childbearing and child raising. Another argument used was that instead of the amendment being used to ensure that labor rights for women would be expanded to include men, the opposite would occur. In other words, working men would lose the rights they had in the workplace as well. In general, though, the opposition was based on different cultural perceptions of gender roles. Most opponents aligned themselves with the argument put forth by Schlafly that the ERA was just an attempt by radical feminists to feminize men and de-feminize women. In reality, the amendment was merely designed to extend to women the rights guaranteed in the Constitution. As far as most women in the counterculture were concerned, the ERA would only state legally what they were already practicing and experiencing in their daily lives.

Chapter 10

Crossing the Atlantic

Most of this book addresses events and aspects of the counterculture in the United States, where the Sixties counterculture is primarily located in historical memory. I think it is essential to augment this memory and look at how the counterculture of the 1970s was played out in other countries, specifically Germany and Italy.

The first concert I paid to go see was at the Kongresshalle in Frankfurt am Main, Bundesrepublik Deutschland. The bands were from Britain. The headliner was the hard rock band Free, perhaps best known for its hit "All Right Now." The other band was a rock-jazz fusion group featuring saxophonist Dick Heckstall-Smith known as Colosseum. The audience looked like rock audiences anywhere, and the drugs were just as abundant as in the US. The next band I saw at the facility was the Rolling Stones. Hundreds of longhaired protesters passed out leaflets attacking the price of the concert tickets while a fair number of police with leashed dogs stood near the gates. A small riot erupted outside the show when people tried to crash the gates. The police and their dogs fought back.

Like most universities in the West, Frankfurt's Johann Wolfgang Goethe Universität campus was the scene of many protests, concerts and other countercultural events. Black Panthers, the rock bands GURUGURU and Amon Düul, Rot Armee Fraktion leader Ulrike Meinhof, and numerous local radicals and leftwing politicians appeared there. The section of the city the university was located in was known as Bockenheim. It was a counterculture haven. Numerous bars and coffeehouses catered to the freak and New Left culture, while communes and student dormitories hung all sorts of banners and flags from their windows. Meanwhile, squatters were beginning to occupy buildings in a neighboring section of the city. The occupiers were a combination of leftwing workers, foreign workers mostly from Turkey and Yugoslavia, university students and unemployed youth. The squats were a response to a housing crunch in the city caused in large part by housing speculators intentionally leaving apartment buildings empty in the hope they could either convert them to much more profitable office space or sell them at a high profit to someone who would. Frankfurt was not the only European city where this phenomenon was taking place. Both West Berlin and Amsterdam's squatting communities were larger and even more established than Frankfurt's in the 1970s.

The squatters applied political pressure on the Social Democrats in the city council to allow the buildings to be occupied and provided with utilities. At the same time, they fixed up the buildings, creating decent living spaces and common areas that included youth centers, schools and even bars. Their desire was to create the world they wanted to live in while politically challenging the one they existed in. Like the freaks in hippie ghettoes and communes across the United States, the Frankfurt squatters wanted to expand their environment on both the physical and spiritual planes. The authorities had other ideas. They ordered the police to clear the buildings. Just as they did in other cities, the attacks by police provoked an intense and violent defense. Over the course of perhaps two years beginning in 1973, the streets of Frankfurt am Main were the scene of fierce battles between police and squatters and their allies. They were also the scene of concerts and street fairs celebrating the squats and the developing Autonomen movement.

A good portion of the militant wing of the German antinuclear movement came out of the squatting movement. Like the Autonomen, (as I touched upon in my discussion of the antinuclear movement), the Green party element, popularly known as Alternativs, derived from the German counterculture. This latter faction was numerically greater than the Autonomen and their fellow travelers. It was also more likely to avoid militant confrontations with the police. Although still more of an extraparliamentary opposition than their McGovernite[xxiv] comrades in the United States, the Alternativs shied away from the more radical lives of the squatters and commune dwellers, while also maintaining a degree faith in the electoral system.

Italy had its own home-grown movements descended from the Sixties counterculture. The most obvious descendants called themselves the Metropolitan Indians. Like the Yippies and other counterculture radicals, the Metropolitan Indians utilized humor, theatre, and outrageousness in their attempt to provoke young people to act. Their existence was in part the result of years of agitation by the Left and anarchists throughout Italian society. It was also in part a reaction to that organizing, which tended to emphasize more traditional cultural values and focused on the primary role the working class was to play in a communist society. This aspect was similar to the New Communist Movement in the United States that saw a preponderance of Maoist and Leninist groups arising from the ashes of the SDS. Most of these US groups also emphasized traditional cultural values, with some going so far as to require couples to get married and rejecting the membership of gay men and women. Naturally, this prudishness clashed with countercultural values, which generally rejected traditional sexual arrangements. The appeal of the Autonomia and ultimately the Indians in Italy was greatest among young workers, students and the occasionally employed youth known in Italian society as "the marginals." This latter group made their living primarily through working day labor jobs and engaging in petty crimes like drug dealing and shoplifting.

The Metropolitan Indians were political yet the politics they presented were often confused and confusing. Given the mainstream position of the Communists in Italian society, the Metropolitan Indians considered them and other mainstream leftwing parties to be part of the problem. Consequently, the Metropolitan Indians opposed not only the capitalist parties but also the organized Left. Although it is possible to make a comparison to the Autonomen in Germany, the Autonomen had a clearer leftist anti-capitalist position and also had a better understanding of the need for cooperation with more traditional Left and liberal grassroots organizations. Both movements insisted on living the revolution they wanted to create and both believed in creating a space to design a revolutionary culture that rejected the dominant themes of work, school and traditional relationships found in both conservative and liberal mainstream culture.

Organized via radio programs and pirate radio stations, the Metropolitan Indians and their allies came together during confrontations with the police, Italian fascists and various reformist Left groups. Italian politics were quite divided at the time. Fascists, encouraged by elements inside the government, completely infiltrated the police forces, using violence and intimidation against the parliamentary and extra-parliamentary Left. The presence of such overt fascism led some leftists to take up armed struggle. Many others chose a path of occupation and confrontation. The Indians were one segment of an ultra-left element that included the national collective Lotta Continua and a number of smaller groups organized in workplaces, universities and high schools, and communes. These groups were collectively known as Autonomia.

The Autonomia began in 1975 when about 100 militants from the far left worker/student group Lotta Continua broke away to set up other autonomous groups, collectives and similar bodies. According to their own writing, they were tired of what they saw as "the seedy little groups of the extra parliamentary Left." Meanwhile, heroin was insinuating itself into the youth ghettoes of the country. Many believed this influx of narcotics to be a conspiracy between the fascists, the police and organized crime that was designed to de-politicize the political counterculture. Later in the year, a national gathering of autonomous groups was organized by the autonomous workers' Via Volsci collective. Among those attending the meeting were a number of anarchists, both affiliated and independent. Among this latter group were the Metropolitan Indians—a group of squatters, students and factory workers with clear countercultural leanings. The idea of calling themselves Metropolitan Indians came about almost by chance. The story is that one evening when members of the group were out painting graffiti someone shouted, "Let's leave the reservation." From that came a series of conversation resulting in the collective choosing to identify themselves as "Indians." They adopted the trappings of Hollywood Indians in their public outings as a means of identification and simply as a joke.

Like the Yippies in the United States, many of the Indians were working class youth who lived in the streets or in urban collectives. Their actions were theatrical in nature and designed to be provocative. Their numbers were small at first, but within a year of their creation, they were drawing thousands to their actions. The participants began to include more and more students and by 1977, the Metropolitan Indians were major players in the student Left.

The Christian Democrat government in Rome had begun to institute university reforms that limited university autonomy and access. In response, small groups of university students in Rome occupied university buildings. Fascist groups staged an armed attack on one such occupation and wounded two of the occupiers. In response, more buildings were occupied.

After the shootings by the fascists, assemblies were held in all the schools in Rome. A demonstration was called against the fascists. During the protest shots were fired, killing a policeman and seriously wounding two students. It was never determined who fired the shots. The fascists had been working with state security forces for years to discredit the Left and anarchist movements. One of their tactics was to set off bombs and blame the Left. The response from the youth of Rome to the shooting was immediate. Soon students, the unemployed, youth from estates on the urban periphery, druggies, gays, and young workers in the underground economy were in the streets. The Metropolitan Indians described the following weeks of protest like this:

> "On demonstrations we cry out: "it's another 1968". "No it isn't '68" Rinascita replies. We say it is another '68 in intention, to underline the desire to turn everything upside down as then and to engage in a process of struggle, which will be broad and powerful, not just a flash in the pan, something off the cuff. At the same time however we are living through a different process. It is much more massive than before, far more radical far more determinedly anti-reformist. Because it is composed of proletari-ans, of people who are already working, have worked already, or are looking for work. It is not reducible to a student dimension. Today, explosion is the continuation of a history begun in April 1975, which has grown throughout '76 eventually broadening out into a movement of young proletarians. The February movement was the conquest of a mass social terrain and the central territory of the university by a subject incarnating the refusal of work."[xxv]

As January turned into February and February into March, more universities were occupied as more students joined the insurrection. Confrontations in the streets between law enforcement and young revolutionaries intensified. Fascist elements and Italian police (Carabinieri) attacked the university occupations and the occupiers fought back. Some protesters began to use guns to fight off the machine guns of the police. Both police and protesters were killed. On March 11, 1977 over 100,000 protesters converged on Rome, fighting police and attacking shops in the rich district of the city. After this protest, the roundups of the radicals intensified, with beatings and torture inside the prisons becoming routine. Radicals that evaded arrest went underground. Some joined the Red Brigades (Brigatta Rosse), an armed group engaged in bank robberies, kidnappings and killing police. Many others just stayed underground or, if they could, left the country. In Bologna, an attempt to disrupt a March 12, 1977

Christian Democrat rally by the Autonomi and other groups on the extraparliamentary Left was attacked by police, resulting in the death of a student from police gunfire. For three days in Communist (PCI)-administered Bologna, the action in the street looked like a revolution. Afterwards, police arrested hundreds, shut down the pirate radio stations, confiscated literature and threw non-PCI publishers on the Left in jail. In May of 1977, several Italian universities and their surrounding neighborhoods remained occupied by protesters. On May 12, 1977 radicals in Rome attempted to hold a protest celebrating the anniversary of a 1974 Italian law legalizing divorce. This was despite a ban on all public protest. The police attacked on all fronts, shooting at protesters and at bystanders hanging out in the street. A woman was shot in the back by police and killed. Protests continued for another three days before the situation settled down. By the end of May, the ban on protests was ended. The movement continued, albeit in a less public way.

The German Autonomen and the Italian autonomous groups (including the Metropolitan Indians) were unique. They actually took the cultural revolution as it manifested itself in those countries, organized it, and turned it into a political revolt. As I noted before, the primary groups that attempted a similar scenario in the United States were the Yippies and their allies the White Panthers, who were not as successful in terms of sheer numbers or in the amount of havoc they created, but were part of the inspiration to some of the elements of the movements in Italy and Germany. Indeed, a line can be drawn between the Metropolitan Indians and the Yippies, if not to any other group. Both groups preferred theatre to organizing and festivals to political rallies. Neither group was afraid of provoking the police, albeit in different ways. While armed struggle in the United States was carried out by underground groups only, the repressive nature of the political situation in Italy in 1977 was such that protesters with guns had become part of the equation at demonstrations and occupations.

The synthesis between the counterculture and the New Left occurred in the United States and Germany around the same time. The combination of police repression against all manifestations of the youth movement and organizing directed at the counterculture by numerous leftist organizations, when combined with the invasion of Cambodia and the murder of six students at Kent State University and Jackson State by authorities in spring 1970 convinced many usually apathetic freaks in the United States to go on strike and fight the police. However, after that wave, the numbers of US protesters tapered off. This was not the case in Germany, where students and working class youth shared not only a countercultural affinity, but also a political one throughout the decade. Italy experienced a similar synthesis, albeit a bit later. The special oppression experienced by youth in all these countries was not only felt differently, but was also responded to differently. Where young people in the United States turned to apolitical pursuits (or joined the various campaigns designed to elect liberal Democrats), the oppositional youth movements in Europe squatted buildings, fought nuclear power and forced the corporate State into crisis.

It's not that youth in the United States were less alienated than their European counterparts. What is more likely is that other social factors were involved. Maybe America's culture of individualism didn't foster a long lasting collective spirit of rebellion that could hold sway in Europe. Maybe the US government was more effective in creating divisions between students and working class dissidents. Maybe the cynicism of the American youth was just too great to overcome.

The Personas of the Counterculture

There is a tendency for observers to insist on separating the political elements of the counterculture from those focused on drugs and music. This approach seems overly simple. Indeed, the synthesis of the two occurred more often than a militant refusal by the adherents of one to involve themselves in the other. Given this, the two personas of the counterculture could be generally classified as the political and spiritual elements. In part because it did not challenge the status quo politically, the latter was able to mutate and survive. It was also coopted. The political elements disintegrated partially because the nature of the counterculture could not sustain a Marxist analysis and also most political organizations that organized among the youth became considerably more doctrinaire in their analyses beginning in late 1968, choosing already defined theories to analyze the situation and trying to force the moment to fit those theories. This was only possible to a certain degree, no matter how creative one's attempts. Of course, the vast majority of youth remained in the 1970s, like their predecessors in the 1960s, pretty apathetic about politics of any kind. Also, they were seeing themselves less and less as part of a counterculture and conversely

Daydream Sunset

also seeing the counterculture as just another form of consumerism. This trend continued as the 1970s wore on and the most consciously oppositional elements of the counterculture diminished in numbers and influence.

Chapter 11

Punks and Glams

Punk rock appeared sometime in the middle of the decade. Like any cultural phenomenon, it is virtually impossible to point to an exact date it began. The poet Patti Smith is often referred to as its godmother. Unlike the manufactured antipathy of the Sex Pistols, who were after all, the brainchild of a clothing store owner, Smith consciously arose from a tradition that could be traced back to the 1960s counterculture and even to the Beats. There was a reason William Burroughs and Bob Dylan both found themselves part of her audience. Her roots in the counterculture were obvious in her references to Bob Dylan, Keith Richards and the Grateful Dead. She made reference to them in interviews, especially in those with the editors of the Yippie newspaper *Overthrow/Yipster Times*. Unlike the punks who rejected the music of the counterculture without necessarily even listening to it, Smith understood punk's roots were in that music. She had gone to Grateful Dead concerts, seen the Rolling Stones and believed in the rebel side of the counterculture and its music. Indeed, it was part of her inspiration. Like previous rock music forms that came from the blues, rockabilly and country, punk would not have come into being if it weren't for the rock music that preceded it. However, most self-respecting punks would only grudgingly acknowledge that fact. Instead, just like rockers before punk, punks insisted on their genre's uniqueness and "newness."

Patti Smith was a child of the 1960s. Never a full-blown hippie, she was obsessed with Bob Dylan and the Rolling Stones. Her use of marijuana and other mood modifiers did not begin until she was in her twenties. After graduating from a southern New Jersey high school in 1964 she got a job in a factory. She became pregnant in 1966 and gave the baby up for adoption in April 1967. Those were typical years for a working class girl in southern New Jersey. They included bus trips up to New York City from her southern Jersey home. These trips involved hanging out in the Village and on the Lower East Side blending into the burgeoning counterculture scene there. She wrote poetry and wore out the groove in her Bob Dylan records. By the end of 1967 she was in New York and had moved in with an artist named

Robert Mapplethorpe. Their lives were storybook tales of starving artists. Both held a series of low-paying jobs, experienced occasional interest in their works and even received some commissions in their chosen fields of art and poetry. By 1973, Smith was performing some of her poems with a small rock band. The band included rock critic and producer Lenny Kaye on guitar, whose *Nuggets* collection of garage rock would become a crucial element of the bridge from Sixties rock to late-1970s punk. By 1975, she had released her first album, *Horses*. She toured the United States and England after its release. It was in England where she was referred to as the Godmother of punk, a musical form just beginning to take shape under that moniker.

Smith was more than just a punk rocker. She was a poet and a rock music fan who had danced at Grateful Dead concerts, consumed the lyrical and musical mastery of Bob Dylan, been infatuated with Brian Jones of the Rolling Stones, and lived with the guitarist for Blue Öyster Cult. Her entry into the rock music world served as a living connection between the established world of rock and the brash, nihilistic punk ethos determined to destroy what it saw as rock's overblown extravagance. Musically, her three chord compositions drew from rock and roll basics that originated with Chuck Berry and were explored by every garage rock band of the 1960s. Lyrically, her songs were poetry of the highest rock and roll order. Her concert audiences were a mix of freaks, punks and literati and her inspirations came from her life, her muses in film and music, and whatever might be happening in the streets.

This latter inspiration is apparent in a 1977 interview she did with the Yippie newspaper *Yipster Times*. To begin with, the fact that Smith chose to have the conversation with this paper gives tangible credence to the argument that Smith's presence was a bridge between the 1960s counterculture and its manifestation in the 1970s. She could have chosen one of the papers geared to the punk scene/community but chose instead a paper representing those who were attempting to maintain a cultural continuity between the two subcultures.

Smith also found fans in the rock scene known as glam. Identified primarily with rockers David Bowie and Lou Reed, this scene sexualized the use of costumes and face painting popular among the hippies. Bowie was the master at this play-acting, creating and discarding personas throughout the 1970s, while Reed wrote and performed tunes that challenged the strictly gendered world most of his listeners were used to. Many fans of the glam genre imitated their favorite performers by dressing up to attend shows and clubs, while those that were the most serious wore a costume every day. The sexual and gender confusion represented by this trend was not only a challenge to the mainstream straight world; it also challenged the generally heterosexual position of the counterculture.

Looking at the phenomenon in a more political way, the gender-bending scene was a form of surrender. By the time David Bowie and Lou Reed had popularized the style, there was an overall cynicism with politics and music with a political message. The general feeling was that the Sixties revolution had failed. So, if one couldn't change the world, why not change one's identity in such a way that was not only radical but said "fuck you" to the powers-that-be and middlebrow America? No class organization was required. This type of change was completely personal and would freak out the people one wanted to freak out. Naturally, to omit the role the gay liberation movement played in this new expression of individual freedom would be naïve. After all, if the images of flamboyant gay men and tough-looking dykes had not arrived in suburban America and Britain, the glam scene may not have taken off like it did, no matter how David Bowie dressed. Regarding glam's political meaning, Dick Hebdige writes in his book *Subculture: The Meaning of Style* that Bowie and the movement he came to represent had virtually no political content. In fact, notes Hebdige, the entire glam movement was, in the end, nothing but an "ambivalent triumph of the oppressed."[xxvi] It liberated individuals from their gender roles, but did little or nothing to liberate their class. Andrew Kopkind, in a review that appeared in the New Left magazine *Ramparts*, discussed glam rock (and Bowie and Lou Reed specifically, calling Bowie's concert the "most flaming" rock performance ever.) Placing the genre in the context of sexual liberation, Kopkind wrote, "if sexuality is just a gimmick...nothing much will change, and the culture will become that more corrupted." He notes that "just as there cannot be truly revolutionary institutions in a non-revolutionary society, there can't be liberated people in a repressive society, only people working on liberation."[xxvii] Although Kopkind wrote these words specifically about the gender-bending rock music of Bowie and Reed, they could easily apply to the whole of the counterculture.

Sexual desire and sexual expression defined much of what the counterculture was about. The eroticism of the rock and roll dance concert was not just imagined. It was as real as the music. The preferred drugs, which meant LSD and marijuana for the most part, were drugs that often increased sexual desire and usually enhanced the actual experience. Once the bonds of monogamy were loosened and the heterosexual sex experience had been tried in multiple ways and with multiple partners, all that remained for those so inclined was to challenge the experience itself. For those who weren't specifically homosexual or specifically hetero, there was bisexuality. For those who did not want to actually have sex with someone of the same gender, but wanted to play around with sexual identity, the world of glam rock made this possible and popular. Rockers like David Bowie, Lou Reed and even Mick Jagger led the way with their lyrics about sexual ambiguity and their dressing up as women/men. Jagger's role in the classic 1971 film *Performance* stretched issues concerning sexuality and sexual identity even further, while simultaneously examining the dying hopes and growing darkness of the Sixties counterculture.

When it came to class issues, both punk and New Left critics scored some points with their criticism of the hippie counterculture. Some of its adherents were wealthy, and, when it came down to it, mostly interested in spending money on hedonistic pursuits. However, most freaks were neither well off or from the upper classes, nor did they necessarily desire to be so. Like almost everywhere else in America, the recession that began in 1973 had heightened the class differences within the countercultural ranks. Indeed, it became clear to the hippies living on the streets and in the woods that their wealthier brothers and sisters buying cocaine and driving nice cars were sharing less. Life on the streets was becoming more desperate as the wealthier hippies kept more of their cash to fund their own passions. Capitalism always feeds greed. Hippies certainly were not exempt from this. Hippie capitalists became less tolerant of those who weren't spending money in their shops and more open to corporate offers to buy them out. Jello Biafra of the San Francisco punk band the Dead Kennedys discussed his experience with hippie capitalism in his hometown of Boulder, Colorado (a mecca for hippie tycoons): "In many ways, I have no idea what would have become of me if punk hadn't happened, because the '70s turned out to be so stale, and so boring, and so backward compared to what had come just before. We were too young to have fully experienced the '60s and the fervor of the anti-war movement. And some of the people who had caused so much trouble for what used to be called the establishment were opening overpriced hanging plant stores on the downtown mall and becoming the early versions of hippie capitalists."[xxxviii]

Biafra's example is a bit hyperbolic, but the essence of it is that the freak counterculture was quickly losing it oppositional character and it was the capitalists who were at the vanguard of this transition. Given this perception and the truth behind it, it was only natural that hippies would be the targets of the punks. Hypocrisy is often easiest to see among those who came directly before. Not all hippies/freaks fell into the category of hypocrite, but enough did to render the punks' charge valid. Furthermore, when punk music began to push its way into the ears of the freaks, its abrasive and often incompetent sound turned off those used to more melodic blues and folk-based sounds. So, for the first few years of punk rock's existence, the lines were clearly drawn. Punks listened to punk rock and hated hippie music and vice versa. Both subcultures hated disco. Of course, there were exceptions to this rule, but in general it held. Like the Sixties counterculture, punk culture was born in the spirit of opposition. However, unlike its forerunner, it was never as influential or popular. Instead, it quickly became just another subcultural genre, like heavy metal. This can be attributed to a number of factors, among which must be included punk's determination to remain exclusive, the aggressive, abrasive nature of the music and the concerts where that music was performed. Unlike the usually mellower nature of most rock shows (unless they were attacked by police or security), punk rock concerts seemed to revel in a certain threat of potential violence, as did their heavy metal counterparts.

Reggae Music

Back in 1969 a fellow named Desmond Dekker put out a single in the United States called "The Isrealites" The song began with the lyric, "Get up in da morning/salving for breaksa...." This was reggae before white people knew what it was. The film The Harder They Come featured a soundtrack of reggae music that highlighted Jimmy Cliff's sound. There were a few other entries on to the US charts in the next few years. Most prominent was Eric Clapton's version of Bob Marley's "I Shot the Sheriff." In 1976, Marley and his band The Wailers were playing colleges across the US and kicking out an hour and a half of music that made the audience dance unlike anything since James Brown or a Grateful Dead show. His band and music had bridged a gap between white and black alterna-

tive culture in Britain. Whether or not this would happen in the United States was questionable, especially considering the much deeper divisions based on race and the greater intensity of racism found there. Interestingly enough, Marley's first real fan base in the United States was mostly white. His band's first concert in the United States took place in Boston, Massachusetts. Very few traditionally Black radio stations played his music at first, while alternative and college FM stations gave him plenty of airplay. By the end of the decade, some college stations featured a regular weekly reggae show. The music would not achieve a truly international popularity until the 1980s, eventually becoming the first (and most popular) of all "world music" forms. Bob Marley would become a symbol of revolution, hope and weed before he died of brain cancer in 1981.

Chapter 12

Media Matters

Underground comix were simultaneously funny, twisted, sexist, anti-sexist, liberating and occasionally just plain sick. The best artists and writers peeled off the layers of hypocrisy, deceit and bigotry prevalent in the mainstream culture. In doing so, they raised the ire of that culture's guardians. Just as ruthlessly, these comix also revealed the shortcomings of the counterculture from which they originated. This was especially true when it came to women. There is no doubt that the drawings and stories of cartoonists like R. Crumb derived from a society riddled with sexism. At the same time, Crumb and other cartoonists' portrayal of society were part of a tradition of satire that includes Jonathan Swift, Marquis de Sade, Voltaire and William S. Burroughs.[xxix] This tradition of satire often works by exaggerating the subject in order to point out its contradictions.

Underground comix survived the 1970s. Many of the poorly conceived ones died out, while some of the better ones mutated artistically and conceptually. New comix, like *Weirdo* and *Anarchy Comix* were published. ZAP comix were always one of the best-selling undergrounds around. So was Gilbert Shelton's Fabulous Furry Freak Brothers series. Both of these titles continued to publish sporadically through the decade. Other titles came and went. Crumb expanded into other art work, at the same that he and other cartoonists began to be acknowledged by the art world. While this was happening, the number of outlets where underground comix were for sale was shrinking. The combination of police and other government harassment, the corporatization of what could be termed the countercultural accessories movement (incense, bongs, rolling papers, etc.), and the gentrification of counterculture neighborhoods caused the closing of hundreds of head shops throughout the nation, where comix were traditionally sold. Usually run by hip capitalists, the shops' need to make a profit limited their ability to withstand the pressures noted above. Consequently, they eventually closed their doors, leaving many consumers of these products in college towns, hippie ghettos and (especially) suburban towns without a place to purchase them.

Anarchy Comics

In the 1970s, underground comix were still published frequently enough so one could get something new every few weeks. Plus, there were always old publications to buy. Sometime in 1978 the first issue of Anarchy Comics was published. A mélange of history, utopian speculation, social commentary and just plain fun, Anarchy Comics were the brainchild of cartoonist Jay Kinney. Previously known for his work with the comic Young Lust and the Bijou Funnies series, Kinney decided to explore his interest in the history and philosophy of anarchism via comic books. When the first issue came out, it sold quickly. In part, this was because of the cartoonists it featured; Spain Rodriguez, Gilbert Shelton (of Austin's Fabulous Furry Freak Brothers), the Frenchman Paul Mavrides, JR Burnham, Epistoliery and Volny on the Kronstadt uprising, Clifford Harper of Britain's Class War Comix, Melanie Gebbies, and Kinney himself. The publisher was none other than Ron Turner, whose dystopian Last Gasp comix foretold a grim future of ecological devastation and human despair.

Over the next ten years, three more issues of Anarchy Comics would be published. Always entertaining and informational, they continued to include most of the aforementioned artists, while adding others along the way, including underground legend Greg Irons and Marvel artist Steven Stiles. Spain's contributions continued to highlight anarchist history: Durruti in the Spanish Civil War and Italy's Roman Spring of 1977; Harper turned his pen to more contemporary social criticism; Mavrides and Kinney collaborated on both. The highlight of this collaboration is the story titled "Kultur Dokuments" that appears in issue number two. This story begins with a tale about a not-too-distant future where the Picto family, depicted with paper-cutouts, lives a two-dimensional life proscribed by the state whose goal is to take over everyone's brain. As the family members succumb, only the teenage son avoids that fate. After being locked into his room by his parents, he finds a comic book that is the best parody of the classic Archie comic series ever published. Titled "Anarchie," it is the story of Anarchie and his friend Ludehead engaged in shenanigans typical of the actual characters except with a twist of rebellion.

Underground newspapers experienced a similar fate. The extreme harassment suffered by some of the more political of these journals is well documented in books like Chicago Seed founder and writer Abe Peck's *Uncovering the Sixties: The Life and Times of the*

Underground Press. Drug busts of the staff and harassment of the printers by police were quite common. Some newspaper offices were firebombed or shot up by right wing gangs or police (and sometimes both). National record companies were pressured by the federal government to end their advertising in the more political papers and newspaper racks containing those newspapers were removed from streets. In addition, the overtly apolitical nature of other counterculture papers inadvertently (or in the case of *Rolling Stone*, quite intentionally) provided advertisers with a "safer" outlet for their copy. Of the underground papers that survived the decade, only the *Berkeley Barb*, *Yipster Times* (which changed its name to *Overthrow*) and a couple others retained their leftist and countercultural editorial policies. Countering this trend, Vancouver, BC's *Open Road*, did not begin until 1976 and published until 1990, maintaining its militant politics until the end. It was founded by former members of Vancouver's Yippies. The rest of the surviving underground papers transformed themselves into local arts and entertainment weeklies that featured reviews, articles and advertising for rock bands and so-called alternative cultural events. When such papers did publish political stories, the political slant was usually a watered down version of their previous perspective. In general, this meant that the anti-imperialist and counterculture left was rarely reported on, while the politicians and movements associated with the extreme liberal wing of the Democratic Party became front and center. This did not mean that there was no longer any good political writing in these papers. Indeed, *Rolling Stone* featured some of the best political writing of its existence during the 1970s when it featured writers like Hunter S. Thompson, Timothy Crouse and Richard Goodwin. However, all of these writers existed within the recently expanded boundaries of US liberal politics—boundaries perhaps best represented nationally by the McGovern presidential campaign of 1972. The left-leaning boundaries of those politics would shrink as the decade progressed. Ted Kennedy's 1980 presidential campaign was the last such left liberal campaign.

Ken Kesey and a few of the Merry Pranksters moved to Oregon in the late 1960s. Tired of police harassment and the increasing acrimony of the scene in northern California, he headed back to the family farm east of Eugene a few months before the Woodstock Festival in August 1969. Some Pranksters did make it to Woodstock and served in a variety of roles beyond mere festivalgoer. The Hog

Farm were a quasi-security force determined to prevent problems before they occurred instead of trying to resolve them after they erupted. Hugh Romney (later Wavy Gravy) was an emcee. Together with the Pranksters, other Hog Farmers prepared food and helped people through bad drug trips.

Kesey had not published even a short article since the bus trip of Furthur made famous in Tom Wolfe's book *The Electric Kool Aid Acid Test*. Back in Oregon, Kesey, his family and some hangers-on lived on a farm between Springfield and Eugene. His brother Chuck ran the family creamery and, together with Chuck's wife, developed a yogurt and kefir that sold well in health food stores and food co-ops. Chuck was also experimenting with growing (and imbibing) psilocybin mushroom cultures. The Grateful Dead played a benefit show (called the Oregon Field Trip) for the Creamery at a fairgrounds outside of Eugene in 1972.[xxx] This concert ranks in the minds of many fans as one of the best concerts the Dead ever played.

Kesey and *Realist* editor Paul Krassner edited the *Last Supplement to the Whole Earth Catalog*. This softcover text appeared in headshops in April 1971. It was published as the April-May issue of *The Realist*, featured a classic cartoon by R. Crumb as its front cover and would be the last supplement to Prankster ecologist (and Buckminster Fullerite) Stewart Brand's *Whole Earth Catalog*. The *Last Supplement* featured several writings by Kesey on a variety of topics including the Chinese oracle I-Ching, the Bible, and dogs. The supplement was a collage of counterculture interests and influences, from baking bread to underground comix to a message from the Weather Underground. In 1974, Kesey began editing a literary journal called *Spit in the Ocean*. This journal featured fiction and poetry from numerous writers associated with the counterculture, including Wendell Berry, Ed McClanahan, and Neal Cassady (who was published posthumously.) He also released a collection of fiction and non-fiction writings under the title *Garage Sale*.

An interview of Kesey by Paul Krassner appears in *Garage Sale*. The interview, originally published in the May-June 1971 issue of Krassner's magazine *The Realist*, covers a wide variety of topics and provides a decent indication of how the counterculture was thinking at the time. It begins with a discussion about guns, racism and revolution. As the conversation progresses, Kesey and Krassner discuss Kesey's books, underground comix, women and liberation, abortion, and Charlie Manson. The book itself ends with a parable about a man who received blowjobs from a breeze and fell in love with that wind. Kesey's frank and seemingly male-oriented literature would spark the ire of some separatist feminists beginning in the late 1970s.

Tom Robbins grew up in Richmond, Virginia, a southern middle-class white boy. After graduating from a military academy, he went on to college and eventually ended up in Seattle, Washington where he wrote about art for the *Seattle Times*. He began the 1960s hitchhiking around the United States. He continued to write about art and music and published his first novel in 1967. That novel, titled *Another Roadside Attraction*, told the story of a band of misfits who discovered the body of Jesus and ran up against a Vatican that had its reasons for getting the body back. The novel is essentially a comic novel that explores issues of religion, spirituality and meaning while reflecting a countercultural sensibility. However, it was his second novel that would make him a countercultural novelist. *Even Cowgirls Get the Blues* is the story of a big-thumbed beautiful hitchhiking young woman and the adventures she has on the road. In the course of the novel, the reader meets a highly sexed philosopher named the Chink who lives in a cave, an effeminate tampon empire CEO who owns a ranch in the US Midwest; the ranchers, who are all women and mostly gay or bisexual, and a flock of whooping cranes. The narrator is Robbins himself and the book, like those that were to follow, serve as a forum for his reflections on such issues as reincarnation, sexual behavior and life in consumer capitalist society.

Dismissed by cynics and others as "hippie novels," Robbins' books were best sellers and often included in college courses discussing the contemporary American novel. Yet, it was among the counterculture hoi polloi that his novels meant the most. Not quite as fundamental to one's "required" reading as *On the Road* or something by Ken Kesey, Robbins' novels were still a common accoutrement in communes, collectives and other living quarters on the hippie side of the counterculture.

Film and theatre are their own unique form of communal experience. Almost always viewed in relatively small venues, especially when compared to a rock festival or political protest demonstration, these formats also require a different form of participation. Although not exactly passive, the ways one involves themselves when viewing a film or play is certainly not the same as the involvement experienced at rock concerts or political protests. However, there is a shared sense of awareness and participation among those who have seen a film or play performed in one of hundreds of venues across the globe. For example, the 1969 film *Easy Rider* was seen by millions in the months following its release and the impact of the film was experienced in a similar manner by every freak or freak-to-be that saw it. Likewise, the experience that was the 1969 Woodstock Music and Arts festival was multiplied a thousand-fold once the film hit movie theatres around the world. The same could be said for the film *Gimme Shelter*, which chronicled the Rolling Stones Altamont fiasco, or the film of George Harrison's Concert for BanglaDesh. In an interesting conflagration of politics, reality, and film, protesters picketed outside of several showings of the Woodstock film in the early weeks of its release. Their complaint was the commercialization of and profiting from the peace, love and music vibe that was used to advertise the event. Meanwhile, in Greece, the ruling military junta banned the film after protests against the regime erupted at theaters showing it.

Two films released in the 1970s about the counterculture presented very different perspectives on the movement are Robert Kramer's 1970 docufiction piece *Milestones* and the 1970 John Avildsen-directed film *Joe*. *Milestones* follows the stories of various members of the counterculture trying to make sense of their lives as they mature into adulthood. It features a war resister just out of prison who is wondering why he went to jail when no one else in his affinity group did. Another scenario deals with a woman about to have a baby and how she plans to care for it while remaining true to her counterculture ways. The entire film is recorded utilizing a Godardesque story approach and camera work that reminds the viewer of home movies, jumpy and occasionally unfocused.

Joe, on the other hand, is a vicious indictment of liberal America that also paints the counterculture as seedy and degenerate. Of all the movies to represent the Sixties in the US, this film is the most unforgiving. For those unfamiliar with the plot, it goes like this: Joe, a loudmouthed working man played by Peter Boyle meets Bill Thompson, a Madison Avenue Brooks Brothers-suited urbane executive, in one of Manhattan's neighborhood bars. Thompson goes to the bar to calm his rattled nerves; he has just killed his daughter's junkie boyfriend in a fit of rage. As the beer glasses empty, it becomes clear to Joe (who has been railing against the counterculture, antiwar protestors and blacks while Thompson quietly drinks) that Thompson has done something Joe only talks about. Thompson has actually killed a hippie. From this moment, an alliance as seemingly unlikely as it is unholy is formed. The story unfolds, with Joe and Thompson entering into each other's lives—lives separated by class, but (as it becomes increasingly obvious) not by politics. The presence of the upper class Thompson in the film differentiates it from its predecessor *Easy Rider*, where the killers are predictable southern rednecks in a pickup.

The final scene is bloody, emotionally explosive, and apocalyptic. Joe and Thompson invade the rural hippie commune where Thompson's daughter lives firing their weaponry. Their killing spree ends only when Thompson does the unthinkable: he murders his daughter in cold blood.

Besides being the nastiest of all the Sixties movies, *Joe* also serves as a metaphor for the political and cultural reality of that period's wake. If Joe represents an American working class driven to bigotry and hatred due to its fear of the changes wrought by the Sixties movements, then Thompson is a stand-in for the establishment culture that felt as under siege as Joe and his compatriots must have felt, albeit for somewhat different reasons. Of course, Joe feared the social changes because he felt he would be left behind, while Thompson opposed them because he feared a loss of status and income. When placed in the larger societal context, the uneasy friendship between the two men in the film easily becomes a metaphor for the political strategy devised by the GOP in 1968 that married the Republican elitist leadership with poor and working class whites.

Another film that attempted to capture the spirit of the time was the animated feature *Fritz the Cat*. Based on the underground comix character originally introduced by R. Crumb in *Zap Comix Number Five*, the film was animated by New Yorker Ralph Bakshi and features Fritz in all his sexist and freak behavior. The film was met by mixed reviews, with establishment critics not exactly understanding the point and some underground reviewers essentially critiquing the cartoon for being a cartoon. Like the comic it was inspired by, there was something in the film to piss everyone off. The failure to appreciate the nature of satire never ceases to amaze those who write it (or draw it) and Bakshi's film was no exception.

Bread and Puppet Theatre

The Bread and Puppet Theatre troupe was birthed in the antiwar protests of the 1960s. Founded by Peter and Elke Schumann, its performances and puppets became a mainstay at antiwar and antiracist protests in New York City and Washington DC during the 1960s. Essentially anarchist, the performances encouraged an erasure of the lines between performer and audience while utilizing ancient Jewish and old European archetypes in their message of peace and justice. The troupe moved to Plainfield, Vermont in 1970 to begin a residency on the campus of the alternative Goddard College. Like many counterculture escapes to Vermont and other rural environs, the early reactions to the troupe were negative. Despite this (or perhaps because of it), Bread and Puppet brought its puppets and message to local events ranging from Independence Day parades to farmer's markets. Eventually, the group bought land in Glover, Vermont and set up shop, putting on the Bread and Resurrection Circus theatre festival every year. They continued to apprentice puppeteers and actors while also sending smaller troupes on tours across the continent and Europe. Their politics remained gently anarchistic, stubbornly satirical and fiercely antiwar.

Chapter 13

Divergence and Synthesis

The 1970s saw the Sixties counterculture diverge into two primary directions. One of these directions was into the mainstream. Rock music, long hair on men, marijuana use, and a greater openness towards sex and sexuality became commonplace. Even the world of sports was affected. Besides the previously mentioned countercultural affinities of basketball player Bill Walton, several baseball players also adopted the lifestyle and some of the ethos of the counterculture. Perhaps the most outspoken of these players was the pitcher Bill Lee. Once, when asked what made him such a good pitcher, he responded by claiming he sprinkled marijuana on his corn flakes every morning. In addition, he expressed support for socialist politics while raising the ire of the Major League Baseball establishment, especially his manager, the crew-cutted, old school Don Zimmer.

While athletes smoked weed and grew their hair long, many other essential elements of the counterculture became less generally accepted. These elements—scamming the system, rejecting work and rent, for example—were still practiced, but only by what might be termed the hardcore freaks. These individuals were mostly found in rural communes and in urban areas that maintained a counterculture vibe and community: neighborhoods like Telegraph Avenue and the Haight-Ashbury. This would suggest that the mainstream culture took the trappings of sex, drugs and rock and roll from the counterculture and rejected its essence and its occasionally extreme politics. In philosopher Herbert Marcuse's 1955 book *Eros and Civilization* he wrote of the potentially liberating aspects that could emerge in what was increasingly considered to be the post-scarcity age. The moment, he wrote, existed for a civilization based on *eros* to come into being. Liberated from the drudgery of survival and work, humanity could make those aspects of the human condition obsolete. In doing so, it could create a society and culture based on a politicized understanding of the Frankfurt School's take on *eros* that emphasized a life truly dedicated to the pursuit of happiness. By 1964, Marcuse had realized that monopoly capitalism could not allow such an approach to exist. Instead, in what can best be perceived as one of the greatest examples of how capitalism mutates and survives to keep and expand its power, US monopoly capitalism took the trappings of the *eros*-based counterculture and turned them into a profit-making machine. Everything that could be commodified was turned into an object for sale and everything else was marked for destruction. The politics of love and ecstasy metamorphosed into instant sexual gratification and drug abuse while the culture's musical celebration grew into a bigger and bigger business.

A less cynical take (and perhaps a more dialectical one) would see the counterculture as the antithesis of the gray-flannel suit culture of the American 1950s and early 1960s. In this dynamic, the partial assumption of that counterculture into the greater culture would be seen as a synthesis of the two, with the advent of punk and hip-hop culture in the late 1970s becoming in turn another antithesis to the incorporation of the counterculture into the mainstream, albeit one not nearly as world-changing or popular. A fine example of the synthesis created between the counterculture and the mainstream culture it opposed can be found in *Rolling Stone*'s coverage of the US presidential campaigns of the 1970s. Its 1972 coverage (especially that of Hunter S. Thompson) had made the magazine's political reporting something to emulate and, more importantly, take seriously. The 1976 Democratic nominee Jimmy Carter understood this quite well. Although a moderate Gerald Ford was the GOP candidate in 1976, the right wing of the party was already in control of the party's future. Former California Governor Ronald Reagan was the man who would carry the right's flag forward (or backward, actually). The GOP continued ignoring the counterculture and its role in US society, putting forth candidates defined by their visceral hatred of the hippies, New Left, and anything that touched them with something besides a nightstick. Carter, meanwhile quoted Bob Dylan and was friends with the Allman Brothers. At the least, he understood the numerical significance of rock music's fandom.

A less glorifying take on the confluence between the Sixties freak cultural politics and mainstream party politics is the one put forth by Yippie Abbie Hoffman in a 1980 *High Times* interview conducted by his co-conspirator Jerry Rubin. While discussing their fellow Chicago Eight/Seven defendant Tom Hayden's election to the California State Senate, Abbie points out that while Hayden was now part of the system, Abbie was a fugitive, having been conned into a cocaine deal by federal agents. Hoffman's point was that there was little room for compromise. Like Black Panther Eldridge was supposed to have said, "You were either part of the solution, or you were part of the problem."

Another arena that saw a synthesis of conventional and counterculture elements appeared in the effort to legalize marijuana. Even the acronym for the primary organization seemed intended to "straighten" out the freaky image associated with potheads. NORML or the National Organization to Reform Marijuana Laws, was founded in 1970 by Keith Stroup with a $5,000 grant from the Playboy Foundation. NORML's primary goal was to change the perception of marijuana and marijuana users in the eyes of those who make the laws. Its secondary focus was to defend those arrested for marijuana possession. Stroup and those involved with the organization consciously cultivated an image of themselves as professional and responsible citizens, hoping to remove the hippie stigma attached to pot. They wore jackets and ties when appearing before the media and legislative bodies and kept their hair modishly short.

I previously mentioned the Robert Kramer film *Milestones*. Originally released in 1975, this film visits counterculture lives in the city and the country, revealing their existence in the wake of their revolutionary commitments (political and cultural) and the changes in that revolution then taking place. Kramer's gritty work is a look at the 1970s through the eyes of a politically inclined member and chronicler of the Sixties counterculture. The essence of the film revolves around the struggle between the needs and desires of the individual and those of the greater group, which in the case of the counterculture was the revolution itself. In short, it does its best to represent what can certainly be argued was the primary battleground of the 1970s, where the individualist US culture fought against the counterculture's communal urgings to restore the selfishness and egotism that is the ultimate realization of American culture.

It's not my nature—nor is it particularly wise—to make grand generalizations about history, especially when the history being considered is relatively recent. I am reminded of the response provided by Chou en Lai to a questioner who asked him what he thought the historical impact of the French Revolution was. Despite the fact that the revolution occurred almost two hundred years prior, Chou En Lai's response was reported to have been, "It's too early to tell." I would have to say the same about the time period I've touched upon in this short book. Nonetheless, it is possible to see the 1970s as a time when the cultural revolution of the 1960s retreated in the face of a vicious and overwhelming attack from the institutions of the dominant culture. This occurred in part because the economics of the revolution ran counter to the profit driven economics of capitalism. The war in Vietnam, while enriching the coffers of certain corporations, was slowly bleeding the rest of the US economy dry. Previous promises of a post-industrial, post-scarcity age where everyone would have shelter, food and education were broken so that the wealthy would never have to exist without the levels of consumption they were used to.

Politically, the rapid transformation of SDS from a broad-based student organization with intentionally vague social-democratic politics to a cluster of super-committed mostly Marxist-Leninist groupings left most student activists without an organization to identify with. In addition, the concerted effort of the left-wing of the Democratic Party (which really was somewhat left wing in the 1970s) to bring young people into its fold further reduced the numbers of youth likely to take to the streets in protest. Indeed, as discussed previously, the last major grassroots protest took place in late April and early May 1971 in what were known as the Mayday protests. After the intense repression of Spring 1970 and the May 1971protests by the Nixon administration, protests against the war and in support of various political prisoners diminished in size and effectiveness.

Perhaps most important, though, was the understanding that Washington had decided it could no longer send young men to Vietnam to fight. The draft continued until 1973, but after 1971, relatively few draftees were sent to fight the war. Inside the military, a state of rebellion existed. Although most GIs were no more political than their non-military compatriots, the affinity for the counterculture and its escapes, combined with their hatred of the war and a justified feeling they were being used, made commanding them difficult. If one adds this to the daily resistance of Black and Latino GIs against the military command structure, it was becoming clear even to the Pentagon that it could not continue to count on keeping the war going with men from the United States. Even in places where open rebellion against the military command did not exist, the lack of discipline that countercultural attitudes encouraged was more than the military's old guard could deal with.

By mid-decade, the counterculture's most committed members

were searching for ways to keep the faith in what was still essentially a youth culture. The institutions of the culture were either closing shop or becoming corporatized. As was briefly noted above, perhaps the best example of the former can be seen in the fate of head shops. These stores, which sold pipes, rolling papers, bongs, underground comix, underground newspapers and other accessories for the pot smoking hippie freak, also served as community centers. Bulletin boards listed ride sharing possibilities, rentals, pets for sale or giveaway, and potential romantic liaisons. In addition, posters for rock concerts, political rallies and meetings, and numerous other events could be found in these shops' windows and on their walls. The shops were usually independently owned and could be found in almost every hippie ghetto in cities and college towns, as well as in some suburban areas. The shops advertised on local hip radio stations and in area underground newspapers. In the town I lived in from 1974-1977, the local headshop was owned by two brothers I grew up with. The shop was named after the Frank Zappa album, The Grand Wazoo. Two other headshops in the area were the Joint Possession and one named after the Bob Dylan song Maggie's Farm. Most of these shops went under because of harassment by the police and landlords combined with much of their merchandise (except for underground comix and newspapers) being picked up and sold by corporate entities like drug stores and mail order shops. In some areas, head shops were bought by corporate concerns and turned into chains of novelty stores. In other locales, they were made illegal. By 1980, there were very few such shops left in the United States, even in places like Berkeley and San Francisco where the counterculture still existed.

As the counterculture continued to face cooptation and attacks, its adherents grew older. Growing up came with other responsibilities, including children. This in itself created a challenge many freaks would eventually find too difficult to surmount. Raising a family is a challenge, especially when attempting to do so outside of entrenched societal forms. Some communal endeavors were able to support children and alternative forms of childrearing, but most couples who wanted to raise children together eventually paired off and assumed some of the dominant culture's approaches. In other words, they got jobs, sent their children to schools and many even got married. This transition did not convert these parents into carbon copies of their parents as much as it altered the nature of the previous concept of family. Women who did not stay with their partners pushed the parameters of a male-dominated system that had always considered single women as problematic at best. This helped change the perception of single parenthood, along with the legal and societal ramifications of divorce. In addition, the greater acceptance of non-traditional sexuality and sexual arrangements would ultimately open the way for less discrimination against gays and lesbians by the decade's end.

Epilogue

I found myself in San Diego, California when 1979 began. Our traveling group of friends had left the environs of Santa Cruz a few months previous because we were told that San Diego had lots of work. Once we got there, of course, we decided that the only work we really wanted was of the temporary variety. Fortunately there was enough of that so if we wanted to work we could. My jobs included two weeks at the El Cajon Buck Knife factory and a month at the Naval Air Station on Coronado Island helping build a computerized mechanism that retrieved parts for fighter planes. Despite its beaches and the city's hip enclave of Ocean Beach, San Diego turned out to be a town of sailors, conservative old people, and a police force full of klansmen. It was not the place for folks like us. Of course, none of us knew this when we arrived except for our friend R, who had spent some time there when he was in the Navy during the war.

In February, Jimmy Carter brought US forces home from Nicaragua and broke off negotiations with the dictator Somoza. The Shah of Iran was trying to find a place to hide his family after being forced to leave Iran in mid-January. His money had already found a place. Elvis Costello played a rapid-fire forty-five minute set in San Diego's Fox Theatre. They were forty-five of the best musical minutes I have ever spent. The band played their entire first album and a rock and roll standard or two barely stopping in between songs. I wanted more, but I don't know if Elvis and the Attractions had any more to give. Rhodesia continued its war against its black inhabitants, despite the growing desire of whites to negotiate a better ending than the one they feared. Afghanistan's left-leaning government was under fire from the mujahedin who were being armed by Washington and Saudi Arabia. This decision would come back to haunt Washington in the years to come.

In early March, after winning a rent strike we had organized, most of us left San Diego separately for the East Coast where we met up at the Union Grove Fiddlers Convention in North Carolina. Sometime while we were en route to the eastern seaboard, the nuclear power plant known as Three Mile Island suffered a partial core meltdown.

The stories from the Nuclear Regulatory Commission and the plant's owners exposed their ignorance (and their assumption of our ignorance as well) in the face of impending disaster. A few days after the fiddlers' convention, the bunch of us went to a Grateful Dead show in Baltimore and—a couple days after that—to a huge antinuclear rally in DC. The Dead performed quite well like they did most of the time in those days. The rally was a bit lukewarm in its politics, but the performance by Bonnie Raitt made it worthwhile. Not long afterwards, we packed up a friend's VW bus and headed west. The route back to the Golden State this time around was through Pennsylvania, Ohio, Indiana, Illinois, Wisconsin, Minnesota, South Dakota and the Badlands. From there we headed into Utah and across Nevada. By the time we reached Winnemucca, Nevada we could almost smell the Pacific and hear its waves calling us home.

We arrived in Berkeley the day after the riots in San Francisco following the verdict for the ex-cop who killed Harvey Milk and Mayor George Moscone. The six of us spent a month or so looking for a place to live. Most landlords rejected any thought of renting to us as soon as they saw our scruffy lot. Eventually, we did find a place. After listening to the landlord, who happened to be the second largest slumlord in the East Bay, tell us how hard it was to be rich, we got the keys and moved in. Six of us crammed in three bedrooms. We weren't a collective so much as a collection of people. We celebrated our new abode with a case or two of malt liquor and a gallon of wine. Bob Dylan's live record from Budokan was the newest album on our playlist. Jimmy Carter made a speech about a national malaise related to Washington's defeat in Vietnam and the corruption and fascist tendencies that had been exposed by the Watergate bust and investigation. The Sandinistas were our new heroes as they fought their way towards an eventual victory in Nicaragua. Nicaragua's malaise was being wiped away by revolution.

A couple months later Somoza fled Nicaragua and the Sandinistas formed the new government in that country. From all appearances, it seemed that the Nicaraguan people were for the most part happy with the change. Unfortunately, the next president of the United States would not share their enthusiasm. In Afghanistan, the US stepped up its support of a predominantly Islamist insurgency.

As the year got closer to its end, Jimmy Carter presented the Carter Doctrine to the world. In essence, this doctrine re-emphasized that Washington would do whatever it took to protect so-called vital resources, especially those of the fossil fuel variety. Consequently, this meant Washington would be increasing its military presence in the Middle East and Persian Gulf regions. Sure enough, within days the Carter administration dispatched the carrier USS Kitty Hawk and a battle group from the Philippines to the Persian Gulf. Moscow responded in its own way by dispatching Soviet troops to Afghanistan to defend its client government in Kabul. The Cold War was heating up again.

A few days before Christmas, while the sounds of Pink Floyd's *The Wall* reverberated in our apartment on Berkeley's Dwight Way, a friend walked in the door with an album from the Clash titled *London Calling*. This album was not only the best punk album of the year. It was the best album, period. From the first cut called "London Calling" to the final cut "Train In Vain," this work had everything a rock album could hope to contain. Rebellion, reggae, and straight-out rock and roll. Armageddon, the street, and the essence of love. When our friends who didn't really like punk took a listen to this album, it changed their minds. Meanwhile, the CIA's war in Afghanistan was beginning in earnest and the revolution in Iran was getting stranger by the week.

Epilogue Redux

The date was January 13, 1980. I was still coming down from a week-long weed, acid and beer-fueled run of Grateful Dead concerts two weeks earlier at the Oakland Auditorium near that town's Lake Merritt Park. No sooner had my brain cells begun to function in this dimension when the word came that the Grateful Dead and a few other musicians were playing an emergency benefit show for a number of refugees fleeing from the killing fields of Cambodia. Although uncertain of the politics behind the event, I trusted the Dead to do the right thing when it came to humanitarianism. Plus, I wanted to go to another concert.

Actually, the situation regarding the Cambodian refugees was not a particularly difficult political challenge. In the wake of the massive bombing campaign conducted by the United States military against the people of Cambodia, a cultish, somewhat Stalinist insurgency known as the Khmer Rouge took power. In the years after that takeover, hundreds of thousands of Cambodians were killed in what seemed like some kind of ritual purging. The post-US war government in Vietnam sent in its army to stem the genocide, yet the killing continued. Eventually, refugees from the bloodshed found their way to Thailand and other countries further from Cambodia. Refugee agencies were overwhelmed. Joan Baez and others folks in the San Francisco Bay Area worked with concert promoter Bill Graham, the Grateful Dead and other musicians to put the concert together.

In another part of the world, fifty-two spies, clerks and other embassy workers were being held by elements of the revolutionary movement in Iran. Despite efforts to negotiate their release, Jimmy Carter's White House was unable to make progress. As later documents seem to prove, this was in large part due to some back door negotiations between far right advisers to GOP presidential candidate Ronald Reagan and the fundamentalist Shia elements in Iran's new revolutionary regime. According to Abolhasan Bani-Sadr, who was the democratic socialist president of the revolutionary government at the time, Reagan's advisers promised to provide the fundamentalist anti-leftist Shia elements under the Ayatollah

Khomeini missile parts and other equipment if they would prevent the release of the hostages before the US presidential inauguration in January 1981. Reagan was convinced that if the hostages were still being held, he could use it to his advantage and get elected. The strategy worked.

There's a song written and sung by the Grateful Dead titled "US Blues." In this tune, Uncle Sam is, in essence, a con-man. PT Barnum and the pot dealer join the medicine man hucksters wearing Carl Perkins blue suede shoes in a rock and roll traveling show. There's a place in the song where the lyric goes, "Shake the hand that shook the hand of P.T. Barnum and Charlie Chan." That night, Jerry Garcia sang the lyric differently. It wasn't Charlie Chan's whose hand was being shook, instead that night Garcia sang, "Shake the hand that shook the hand of P.T. Barnum and the Shah of Iran." A friend standing next to me was wearing a t-shirt advertising Oakland's Major League Baseball team the Athletics, known familiarly as the A's. It was definitely not an official shirt since the gold letters on the green shirt read "The Fuckin' A's." He handed me a pipe filled with DMT. The 1980s had begun.

An Introductory Bibliography
Books

(By no means complete, this bibliography serves as a useful beginning.)

Auther, Elissa;Lerner, Adam. *West of Center : Art and the Counterculture Experiment in America*, 1965-1977. Minneapolis, MN. University of Minnesota Press. 2012

Bani Sadr, Abu Al-Hasan. *My Turn to Speak: Iran, the Revolution and Secret Deals With the U.S.* Brassey's Inc. 1991

Boal,Ian, Stone, Janferie, Watts, Michael, and Winslow, Cal, eds. *West of Eden: Communes and Utopia in Northern California*. Oakland, CA. PM Press. 2012.

Brightman, Carol. *Sweet Chaos: The Grateful Dead's American Adventure.* New York. Random House. 1999

Carlsson, Chris, ed. *Ten Years That Shook the City*. San Francisco. City Lights. 2011

Compost, Terri. *People's Park, Still Blooming*. Berkeley. Slingshot. 2009

Crown, Sheryl. *Hell No We Won't Glow*. London. Housman's. 1979

Davis, Angela, et al. *If They Come in the Morning*. New York. Signet. 1972

Edwards, Phil. *More work! Less pay!: Rebellion and Repression in Italy*, 1972-1977. Manchester, U.K. Manchester University Press. 2010

Estren, Marc J.. *A History of Underground Comics*. Berkeley, CA. Ronin Books. 1993

Geronimo. *Fire and Flames: A History of the German Autonomist Movement*. Oakland, CA. PM Press. 2012

Grogan, Emmett. *Ringolevio: A Life Played for Keeps*. Boston. Little, Brown. 1972

Hebdige, Dick. *Subculture: The Meaning of Style*. London. Routledge. 1979

Hoffman, Abbie. *Soon to Be a Major Motion Picture*. New York. Putnam. 1980

Holmstrom, John & Hurd, Bridget; eds. *Punk : The Best of Punk Magazine*. HarperCollins Pub. 2012.

Jackson, George. *Soledad Brother: The Prison Letters of George Jackson*. Chicago Review Pr. Chicago. 1994

Katsiaficas, George. *The Subversion of Politics: European Autonomous Social Movements and the Decolonization of Everyday Life.* Oakland, CA. AK Press. 2006

Kesey, Ken. *Garage Sale.* New York. Viking Press. 1973

Mungo, Raymond. *Total Loss Farm: A Year in the Life.* New York. E.P. Dutton 1970

Nocenti, Annie and Baldwin, Ruth, eds. *High Times Reader,* New York. Nation Books. 2004

Peck, Abe. *Uncovering the Sixties: The Life and Times of the Underground Press.* New York. Pantheon Press. 1985

Raskin, Jonah *Revolution For the Hell of It.* Berkeley, CA. University of California Press, 1998

Robb, John. *Punk Rock: An Oral History.* PM Press. Berkeley, CA. 2012

Robbins, Tom. *Even Cowgirls Get the Blues.* New York. Houghton Mifflin. 1976

Roberts, Andy. *Albion Dreaming: A Popular History of LSD in Britain.* Marshall Cavendish Limited. 2008

Shulman, Bruce. *The Seventies: The Great Shift In American Culture,* Society, And Politics. New York. Da Capo Press. 2002

Stewart, Sean. *On the Ground: An Illustrated Anecdotal History of the Sixties Underground Press in the U.S.* PM Press. Berkeley. CA. 2011

Stimeling, Travis D. *Cosmic Cowboys and New Hicks: the Countercultural Sounds of Austin's Country Music Scene.* New York. Oxford University Press. 2011

Thompson, Hunter S. *Fear and Loathing in Las Vegas.* New York. Random House. 1971

Thompson, Hunter S. *Fear and Loathing on the Campaign Trail* 1972. New York. Random House. 1973

A Very Brief Discography

(Also not complete, these are what I consider the most important albums of the 1970s as regards the intention of this book.)

Allman Brothers. *Live at the Fillmore East 1971. Eat a Peach 1973. Brothers and Sisters 1973. Live at the Atlanta International Pop Festival: July 3 & 5, 1970, 2011.*

The Band. *The Band 1969. Stage Fright. 1971. Rock of Ages. 1972*

Beatles. *Abbey Road. 1969; Let it Be. 1970*

Browne, Jackson. *For Everyman*. 1973. *Late For the Sky*. 1974; *The Pretender. 1977*

The Clash. *The Clash*. 1976. *Give 'Em Enough Rope*. 1977. *London Calling. 1979*

Cliff, Jimmy, et al. *The Harder They Come*. 1972.

Crosby, Stills, Nash & Young. *Déjà Vu* 1970. *Four Way Street* 1972. "Ohio/Find the Cost of Freedom." 1970.

Dead Kennedys. "California Uber Alles." 1979. *In God We Trust, Inc.* 1980

Desmond Dekker. "Israelites." 1969

DOA. *Something Better Change*. 1980.

Dylan, Bob. *Nashville Skyline* 1969. *Self-Portrait* 1970. "George Jackson" 1971. *Planet Waves* 1974. *Blood On the Tracks* 1975. *Desire* 1976. *Bootleg Series Live* 1975. *Street Legal.* 1978. *Slow Train Coming*. 1979.

Elvis Costello and the Attractions. *My Aim is True* 1978

Gang of Four. *Entertainment.* 1978

Grateful Dead. *Workingman's Dead*. 1970; *American Beauty*. 1970; *Skullfuck*. 1971; *Europe '72.* 1972 *Wake of the Flood*. 1973; *Mars Hotel* 1974; *Blues for Allah* 1975

Hendrix, Jimi. *Band of Gypsys*. 1970

Lennon, John. *Plastic Ono Band*. 1970

Lynyrd Skynyrd. *Lynyrd Skynyrd* 1974. *One More From the Road* 1976

Marley, Bob. *Natty Dread*. 1975; *Live!* 1976

Nelson, Willie. *Red Headed Stranger.* 1975

Patti Smith Group. *Horses* 1975. *Radio Ethiopia* 1976. *Easter* 1977. *Wave* 1978

Rolling Stones. *Let it Bleed* 1969. *Sticky Fingers* 1970; *Exile On Main Street* 1971. *It's Only Rock and Roll* 1975. *Some Girls* 1977.

Sex Pistols. *Never Mind the Bollocks* 1977.

Sly and the Family Stone. *There's A Riot Going On* 1971.

Various Artists. *Woodstock*. 1970

Articles

Cowan, Suzanne. "The Unhappy Adventures of 'Alice' in Blunderland." Radical America. vol. 11, no. 6; vol. 12, no. 1. pps. 67-77. 1978

Flippo, Chet. "Willie Nelson and the Austin Scene." *Popular Music and Society.* Volume: 6, 1979, 280-83.

Holden, Stephen. "Jackson Browne Late For The Sky." *Rolling Stone.* Nov. 7, 1974

Kopkind, Andrew. "Gay Rock: The Boys in the Band." *Ramparts.* March 1973

Maslin, Janet. "Jackson Browne For Everyman." *Rolling Stone.* Nov. 22, 1973

Resin, David. "Jackson Browne: Such a Clever Innocence." *Crawdaddy.* January 1974

Thompson, Hunter S. "Fear And Loathing On The Campaign Trail '76 Third-Rate Romance, Low-Rent Rendevous." *Rolling Stone.* June 3, 1976

Films

Easy Rider. Hopper, Dennis. Columbia. 1969

Gimme Shelter. Maysles, Albert. Maysles, David. Zwerin, Charles. Cinema 5. 1970

The Harder They Come. Henzell, Perry. 1972

Joe. Avildsen, John G.. MGM. 1970

Milestones. Douglas, John. Kramer, Robert. Cinegate. 1975.

Renaldo and Clara. Dylan, Bob. 1978

Sunshine Daydream (Veneta, Oregon 1972) Grateful Dead. 1972

Woodstock. Wadleigh, Michael. Warner Brothers. 1970

Journals and Magazines

By no means a complete listing of periodicals (especially underground newspapers), I have listed those mentioned or used for background in the text.

Berkeley Barb. Berkeley. CA.

Crawdaddy. New York

Diamondback. College Park, MD.

Grassroots. Berkeley, CA

High Times. New York

International Times. London, UK.

Oz. London, UK.

Ramparts. Berkeley, CA.

RAT. New York

Rolling Stone. San Francisco, CA./New York

Quicksilver Times. Washington, DC

Village Voice. New York

Washington Area Spark. Takoma Park, MD.

Yipster Times/Overthrow. New York

Websites

Green Mountain Communes: The Making of a Peoples' Vermont
http://sixties-l.blogspot.com/2008/01/green-mountain-communes-making-of.html

Memories of a Metropolitan Indian. http://www.revoltagainstplenty.com/index.php/archive-global/35-memories-of-a-metropolitan-indian.html

End Notes

i. Kopkind, Andrew. "Gay Rock: The Boys in the Band." Berkeley, CA. Ramparts. March 1973. pps 49-51

ii. Thompson, Hunter S. Fear and Loathing in Las Vegas. New York. Random House. 1971

iii. Morrison, Jim. Krieger, R. from the song "Five to One." Originally released as the B side of "Light My Fire."

iv. Wolfe, Tom. "The 'Me' Decade and the Third Great Awakening." New York Magazine, August 23, 1976

v. The debate took place in the pages of the London underground paper The Black Dwarf between Lennon and New Leftist John Hoyland who wrote for the paper. In essence, the argument was over the course of the revolution. Should we free our minds or the institutions? White Panther John Sinclair had the best answer: why not both?

vi. McClanahan, Ed. "A Brief Exegis of Certain Socio-Philosophical Themes in Robert Hunter's Lyrics to 'New Speedway Boogie.'" Last Supplement to the Whole Earth Catalog/The Realist. April-May 1971

vii. The most straightforward definition of the term in this usage comes from the Hippie Dictionary. It reads, "freak (is) a self-denigrating term used by hippies to describe themselves. Early on, the hippie counterculture was characterized as "a freak of society" by the straight culture, so, in defiance, hippies adopt the word freak and used it themselves." (John Bassett McCleary, The Hippie Dictionary. Random House NY 2004)

viii. Jefferson Starship was primarily Grace Slick and Paul Kantner's band. Their first two album, Blows Against the Empire and Sunfighter featured a cast of California rockers that included Jerry Garcia, Joni Mitchell, and David Crosby among others. Red Octopus was a pop-oriented disc that featured a group of musicians who would play as Jefferson Starship for several years.

ix. Rosenbaum, Ron. "Please Don't Take My Sunshine Away." Village Voice. June 24, 1971

x. In Britain, however, one of the biggest LSD production and sales projects ever was just getting underway. Responsible for distributing at least a million doses of LSD, the conspiracy would finally be broken up by British police (after more than a year of surveillance) in 1977.

xi. The letter appears here http://www.konformist.com/1999/leary.htm

xii. Rosenbaum, Ron., "Interview: Michael Kennedy." High Times. January 1977.

xiv. Once, while attending one of Willie's Fourth of July Picnics I was handed a card inviting me to a KKK rally outside of Sacramento, California. My friend Robert Huff told the recruiters to go to hell. They looked at him like he was crazy and asked him if he hated white people. His response was "only racist ones."

xv. It remains questionable how much Clapton actually modified these views. His clarification over the years was that he was not racist, but also thought Powell made some good points regarding immigration.

xvi. Bowie later retracted and apologized for his statements, telling an interviewer: "I have made my two or three glib, theatrical observations on English society and the only thing I can now counter with is to state that I am NOT a fascist." From Melody Maker. October, 29, 1977.

xvii. LSD dealers and manufacturers in Britain would go on to help spawn the free festival culture in the United Kingdom that existed until 1980.

xvii. Mankin, Bill. "We Can All Join In: How Rock Festivals Helped Change America." Like the Dew. March 4, 2012

xviii. Van Deusen, David. "Green Mountain Communes: The Making of a Peoples' Vermont." Catamount   Tavern News Service, Northeast Kingdom, VT

xix. Ibid.

xx. Morgan, Robin. "Goodbye to all that." New York. The Rat: All Women's Edition. March 31, 1970 reprinted from The Word of A Woman: Feminist Dispatches (2nd edition), W.W. Norton, Copyright 1970, 1994.

xxi. Simpson, Bob. "Cock Rock: The Rape of Our Culture." Takoma Park, Md. Washington Area Spark October 2, 1972.

xxii. Van Deusen, David. "Green Mountain Communes: The Making of a Peoples' Vermont." Catamount Tavern News Service, Northeast Kingdom, VT

xxiii. Lemke-Santangelo, Gretchen. Daughters of Aquarius: Women of the Sixties Counterculture. Lawrence, KS. University Press of Kansas. 2009 p. 159

xxiv. This refers to supporters of the counterculture supporters of the ultra-liberal 1972 Democratic presidential candidate George McGovern.

xxv. Memories of a Metropolitan Indian. http://www.revoltagainstplenty.com/index.php/archive-global/35-memories-of-a-metropolitan-indian.html Accessed September 15, 2013

xxvi. Hebdige, Dick. Subculture: The Meaning of Style. Routledge. London. 1979 p. 62

xxviii. Kopkind, Andrew. "Gay Rock: The Boys in the Band." Berkeley, CA. Ramparts. March 1973. pps 49-51

xxviii. Vander Mollen, Jodi. "Jello Biafra Interview." The Progressive. Madison, WI.. February 2002.

xxix. For an in depth discussion of the history and meaning of underground comix, see Mark J. Estren's A History of Underground Comix (Ronin Books) and cartoonist Denis Kitchen and James Danky's Underground Classics Transformation of Comics into Comix (Harry Abrams 2009).

xxx. The fairgrounds referred to later became the site of the Oregon Country Fair, a counterculture festival that occurs every summer. It was also the site of a second Grateful Dead headlined concert in 1982. That concert was called the Second Field Trip.

Thank You

Thanks to Jeffrey St. Clair for suggesting I write this. Thanks also to Holly and Ian Thistle for their critique and comments regarding subject matter and analyses. Michael Breiner's suggestions about matters such as the importance of different topics were crucial to my approach to the text. Peter Bohmer's synopsis of the economic situation in the 1970s was extremely useful in helping to contextualize the period. Kristin Hindes and Naomi King of St. Michael's College InterLibrary Loan Department made my research just plain easy. Of course, thanks to my family, especially Hannah for her ever-cheerful presence. And thanks to Counterpunch.

Besides the people mentioned already, this book is the result of lived experience, standard and not-so-standard research, and numerous conversations and online exchanges over the years between participants in the counterculture, readers of the manuscript and myself. These folks include (but are not limited to) Jay Moore, Roz Payne, Robert and Patti Huff, Will Miller, (Hog Farm) Richie Shirley, Daniel Lewis, Marc Estrin, Richie Moss, the members of the Route One Brigade Facebook Page, David Abeles, Debra Monaghan, Michael Day, Martha Day, Chip Sommers, Wendy and Amy Bardsley, Vincent Boley, Bonnie Resnick, and the Sixties-L listserv.

Note: In the period discussed, the term "straight" referred not only to one's sexuality, but could also refer to one's cultural and drug preferences. A hippie/freak could be straight sexually, but not straight otherwise.

The selection from "Goodbye To All That..." by Robin Morgan is reprinted by permission from Robin Morgan's collection of essays *The Word of A Woman: Feminist Dispatches (2nd edition)*, W.W. Norton, Copyright 1970, 1994. All rights reserved.

The quote from "Green Mountain Communes: The Making of a Peoples' Vermont." Is reprinted by permission from David vanDeusen, Catamount Tavern News Service, Northeast Kingdom, VT. 2009.

Index